Supervision and Coaching

CU00657027

What is supervision, and what is distinctive about supervision for coaches?

This book has a dual purpose: to explore the value of supervision to both giver and receiver in a transformative relationship, and to offer practical guidance for both beginning and experienced supervisors.

In *Supervision and Coaching*, Hilary Cochrane and Trudi Newton create a story of supervision, beginning with a challenge: how can we find an understanding of what happens in supervision, and what is it that we do that enables learning in this relationship to be both a source of professional growth and personal development? The authors identify what goes on in the process of supervision, whatever the field of application, and look at the role of being a supervisor as separate and different from being a master practitioner or mentor. With clarity and through real-life examples, the book explores the relationship and the developmental impact of supervision, using transactional analysis and other models to understand and discuss its psychological basis. *Supervision and Coaching* includes current theories of adult learning and sections on creating effective contracts, supervision with groups and working as an external supervisor for internal coaches.

Combining practical guidance for both beginning and more experienced supervisors with reflection on the underpinning 'roots' of supervision, *Supervision and Coaching* will be an essential resource for coaches in practice and in training, coach supervisors and other professionals working in a supervisory role.

Hilary Cochrane has been a leader in the field of coaching and coach supervision for more than 20 years. She supervises, coaches and develops individuals, groups and teams both in organisations and working independently.

Trudi Newton is an educational trainer and supervisor in transactional analysis with a passion for supervision as a resource and means of co-created learning. She works worldwide in a wide range of learning contexts, including as a coach supervisor.

Supervision and Coaching

Growth and Learning in Professional Practice

Hilary Cochrane and
Trudi Newton

Routledge
Taylor & Francis Group

LONDON AND NEW YORK

First published 2018
by Routledge
2 Park Square, Milton Park, Abingdon, Oxon OX14 4RN

and by Routledge
711 Third Avenue, New York, NY 10017

Routledge is an imprint of the Taylor & Francis Group, an informa business

© 2018 Hilary Cochrane and Trudi Newton

British Library Cataloguing in Publication Data
A catalogue record for this book is available from the British Library

Library of Congress Cataloguing in Publication Data
Names: Cochrane, Hilary, author. | Newton, Trudi, author.
Title: Supervision and coaching: growth and learning in professional practice / Hilary Cochrane, Trudi Newton.
Description: New York: Routledge, 2018. | Includes bibliographical references and index.
Identifiers: LCCN 2017025615 (print) | LCCN 2017038669 (ebook) | ISBN 9781315268156 (Master e-Book) | ISBN 9781138287730 (hardback) | ISBN 9781138287747 (pbk.) | ISBN 9781315268156 (ebk)
Subjects: LCSH: Supervision. | Executive coaching. | Educational psychology. | Transactional analysis.
Classification: LCC HM1253 (ebook) | LCC HM1253 .C63 2018 (print) | DDC 658.4/07124–dc23
LC record available at https://lccn.loc.gov/2017025615

ISBN: 978-1-138-28773-0 (hbk)
ISBN: 978-1-138-28774-7 (pbk)
ISBN: 978-1-315-26815-6 (ebk)

Typeset in Times New Roman
by Deanta Global Publishing Services, Chennai, India
Printed and bound by CPI Group (UK) Ltd, Croydon, CR0 4YY

Contents

Figures

Tables

Abbreviations

EATA	European Association for Transactional Analysis
EMCC	European Mentoring and Coaching Council
IARTA	International Association for Relational Transactional Analysis
ICF	International Coach Federation
TA	Transactional Analysis
TAJ	Transactional Analysis Journal

Acknowledgements

The coaching world is a lively and enthusiastic place, and we have been privileged to work with many colleagues who have inspired us and helped us to develop our ideas. Within that world, we have especially engaged with those who believe in – and want to extend – supervision as a significant part of coaching. Several of these people have contributed to the realisation of this book – too many for all of them to be named, but there are some who deserve special mention:

Our colleagues and co-workers, Delscey Burns, Margot Corbin and Jane Emmanuel, have not only encouraged and supported us throughout the process of writing this book, but have allowed us to test out our ideas on them – and steal ideas from them: thank you, and we hope our long association will continue to spur us on in the future!

Thanks also to Patrick Hobbs for the quote in Chapter 2 and for the flow model in Chapter 3; to Doug Hampson for the continuing revelations of the tactile imagos initiative; to Alistair Nee for his version of the seven-eyed model (which we have further adapted to make eight-eyed); to Pippa Bassan, Diane Clutterbuck, Sarah Gornall, Leda Turai, Georgina Woodstra, and the Surrey Group for sharing experiences with us.

Special thanks must go to two people: Colin Brett, for bringing us together in a creative partnership ten years ago – and for his continuing friendship; and, more recently, Pat Marum for support (and reading our text) – a real 'trusted critical friend'.

Our workshop participants have contributed in significant ways: listening, responding, stimulating and forcing us to look at our own ideas and viewpoints – and ask ourselves questions. For all this, and for so much positive encouragement and inspiration, thanks to you all! We are also delighted to be able to include some of the haikus, poems and insights created during the workshops.

A big thank you to our supervisees who have all, in their many different ways, taught us a great deal about supervision – and about ourselves. We have enjoyed so many enabling, engaging and creative professional relationships even, or especially, at those times when we felt challenged.

We are grateful to many transactional analysts who have enthused us about various aspects of supervision from Mary Cox and Sue Eusden we have borrowed and developed ideas from their articles in *Transactional Analysis Journal*. Rosemary Napper, as colleague and friend, has shared many ideas – especially about supervision as a learning process. Evelyne Papaux opened our minds to the distinction between supervision and practice analysis – an invaluable addition to our thinking. Charlotte Sills and Marco Mazzetti gave visual meaning to our sense of supervision in their diagrams – which we have developed and drawn on to suit the present text.

Some writers have been important in forming our thinking and our philosophy over the years. Two of whom we specially want to thank for their influence are Carl Rogers and Paulo Freire.

We wish to thank Sage Publications for permission to use two diagrams:

'Major Phases of an Individual's Developmental Time Clock' in Levin-Landheer, Pamela (1982) 'The Cycle of Development' *Transactional Analysis Journal* 12: 129–39 (Figure 2.1);

'The Positive Triangle of Social Rôles' in Le Guernic, Agnès (2004) 'Fairy Tales and Psychological Life Plans', *Transactional Analysis Journal* 34: 216–22 (Figure 2.4);

and Stylus Publishing for the diagram of the transformation line –

reprinted from *The Art of Changing the Brain: Enriching the practice of teaching by exploring the biology of learning,* by James E. Zull (Sterling, VA: Stylus Publishing, LLC) with permission of the publisher, Copyright © 2002, Stylus Publishing, LLC (Figure 4.4).

We could not have completed this book without the support and belief in us shown by our partners, Gilbert Cochrane and David Newton – and appreciative thanks to David also for bringing it all together, editing, creating the diagrams, preparing the text, for teamwork and collaboration throughout the project.

Thanks also to Susannah Frearson and Elliott Morsia at Routledge for their encouragement, patience and practical help.

Finally, a big thank you to everyone in the coaching and the transactional analysis worlds – and especially to those who care about supervision – for all we have learnt, and for the continuing discourse, which means that all of us together really can make more of a difference.

Introduction

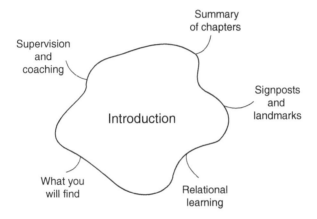

Learning is a meeting point between intentionality and surprise.[1]

What makes supervision special? Why is it different from other relationships? And what is particularly distinctive about coach supervision?

These are the questions we were asking ourselves in a kitchen in Portugal, as we prepared supper with a group of coach supervisors taking part in a residential workshop in the spring of 2015. The group had been working together for nearly five years, teasing out the issues we encountered in our practice and learning. Being together for a few days as a small community, sharing the same space and ethos, cooking and eating together in a fresh, peaceful and beautiful environment, we had lots of time to pool our discoveries as we asked, 'What are we talking about when we talk about supervision?'

We began to realise that our practice as coaches was changing: the experience of becoming a coach supervisor meant becoming a better coach – the reflective approach involved in supervising others is valuable for the supervisor as well. And we wanted to explore more than simply, 'how to do supervision and how to be effective'. As we talked about what we were learning and how we were learning it, bringing together our resourcefulness and experience, we found we were creating something new and significant for ourselves, for the coaches we work with and for their clients.

We are all creating a new paradigm as we go: 'We make the road by walking'.[2]

Coaching is a relatively new field of 'people work', and supervision within the coaching profession is even more recent. Understandings of coach supervision are still very varied (in one recent survey, nearly half of respondents claimed to use a peer arrangement for their supervision; the same study showed that in the USA less than half of coaches have any form of supervision on their work[3]).

Professional supervision for coaches has often been a choice between business consultancy and psychotherapy-based models. Both of these have their value, but our intention in our work and in our writing is to develop something different: first by answering the general question of what supervision is, and then by identifying what goes on in the process of supervision – in all its fields of application. We also consider the role of supervision to be distinct from being a master practitioner or mentor.

So this book is not just about coaching and supervision in practice; it is about the internal changes that happen, for ourselves and others, and how we deal with them. It is not only about the 'function' of being a supervisor, but about the process of becoming a supervisor; not just the learning involved, but the internal growth, the shift in focus, that enables the supervision relationship to be a resource, a model, or even sometimes a refuge and a safe haven for others.

We have a dual purpose: to go beyond a sociology of supervision to explore its ethos, the 'story behind the story', and to offer practical guidance for both beginning and experienced supervisors: a philosophy of supervision with practical guidance embedded within it. At the same time it will become, we hope, a biography of a profession in development.

Where are we coming from?

Part of this 'biography' lies in thinking about what we have learnt since we became engaged in training coach supervisors. All that follows has been developed out of training courses and professional development groups that we have designed and delivered in the UK, Portugal and South Africa over the last ten years.

Our own practice as supervisors, the ideas we developed for use with coaches as well as other people-work professionals, led us in 2011 to self-publish a resource manual for coach supervisors.[4] Further thinking, more practice (and the many reflective responses of our students and supervisees) has resulted in us deciding to move beyond the 'how' of coach supervision to 'why we do it – and why this way'.

The two of us come from very different professional backgrounds. To introduce ourselves: Hilary works widely in the corporate arena as a coach and as a supervisor with individuals, groups and teams. Trudi is an educational transactional analysis supervisor and trainer, working worldwide in a wide range of learning contexts, including as a coach supervisor, while focusing on writing and research. We met on the first coach supervisor training programme that Trudi ran, and have worked together in many different ways since then. Both of us are passionate about working co-creatively to develop what we see as the power for change and beneficence in supervision.

Increasingly, the good news of the last few years is that supervision for coaches has been much more widely thought about, debated and accepted. There is now quite a lot of development going on in the field; this is a reason for us continuing to develop our thinking, co-creating with each other and with those we've trained, getting stuff back 'into the system' for an immediate and positive impact.

Where are we heading?

As we 'make the road by walking', we have found a few signposts on the way:

How we work is who we are

This is important for our thinking: what we can most powerfully offer our supervisees is a relationship with a real person; someone who is present, alive, responding emotionally and intellectually, using themselves in the service of the work … very firmly and clearly working out current and real issues in as straight, effective, honest and caring a relationship as is possible (Shmukler 2010).[5]

The more clearly we can be ourselves, the more we can bring this quality to the relationship; a relationship in which we can assume that this is a place

- of possibility and safety, without personal judgement; where learning is noticed and recognised and competence is brought into awareness;
- where both partners can be truthful; where there is joy in learning and no shame of disclosure;
- where there is an authentic collegial relationship, a balance of power, and both parties are absolutely accepted.

The dialogue between courage and vulnerability

Supervision means developing as a professional within a learning relationship that has at its heart courage and vulnerability, in equal measure on both sides. The truth of this understanding emerges from the responses we've had: 'I can learn without feeling bruised', 'I've learnt so much, but haven't gone away feeling ashamed', 'it was such fun – we laughed a lot – how amazing is that!' … and so on.

The value of not saying much

A more recent signpost shows us how much we've learnt about not saying much – and the impact of silence on self and other. Recognising that we are highly skilled and professional doesn't mean we have to have all the answers!

Sometimes we need to be asking ourselves:

- What am I doing?
- By what right?
- How am I doing it?
- And why?

Be patient toward all that is unsolved in your heart and try to love the questions themselves ...[6]

Relational learning

This interrogation of experience and learning leads to an exploration of 'what goes on' in supervision when it is seen as relational learning – as a connectedness, beneficial not only to participants but to the wider context: a positive approach that demonstrates a belief in people and persons, and – beyond self – a dynamic that ultimately ignites, sustains and gives meaning to the work that we do.

Supervision demands a shift from isolation and stasis to connectedness and development; a process of continual, shared, spiritual reflection.[7] We want this approach to permeate all we do, teach and write about while staying aware that people sometimes need information, guidance and protection.

As you will see in the chapters that follow, we believe in supervision as an equal (not a top-down) relationship: in itself, the term 'supervision' is questionable – it can imply control or management. Some writers prefer the term 'consultation', emphasising a peer relationship where both parties bring their own observations and skills to the process, reflecting the desirability of ongoing professional learning, questioning and support (Cornell & Shadbolt 2007).[8]

While this is close to our own thinking, we still call both the process and the relationship we are describing 'supervision': first, because the term is in general use in the coaching world, but also because we want to address 'beginning' as well as more experienced supervisors – and those engaged in the development of less experienced coaches.

Understanding supervision

In this book we are looking at the philosophy, the theory and the working practices of a profession which is still in a highly volatile developmental phase. For example, there is not, as yet, any agreement between the major professional bodies which represent supervisors on the definition of what a supervisor is or what supervisors do. We therefore invite you to enter into a dialogue with us: to accept the challenge to think about what we want to achieve in this emerging profession, what our hopes and expectations are for its continuing development.

Having said that, we are clear that the particular path we are on has some fundamental, underpinning beliefs. Our view of supervision can be described in several ways, which are also a collection of the principles that we adopt:

A co-creative approach

We have learnt a lot from an approach that is present-focused, that engages all parties in the exchange and development of ideas, and understands that, in doing this, we are together making something new – a truly co-creative practice. It is the opposite of the deterministic attitude that says, 'This is how it has to be.'

In 'What is supervision?' (Chapter 1), we give an overview of supervision: our own perspectives and ways of working. We consider supervision in different fields with a focus on coach supervision, its particular context and requirements. This offers a practical approach to the 'why and how' of co-creative supervision and the person of the supervisor, and sets the scene for the chapters that follow.

We will distinguish supervision from mentoring, mentor coaching, counselling, consultancy and practice analysis, looking at their similarities and differences; each of them has an important place in the coaching world, but in this book we consider the role of supervision in locating how and where 'the personal intrudes into the professional' – and how this relates to a supervisee's growth and needs.

A psychological base

All kinds of 'people-work' can benefit from a framework for understanding what goes on for us and between us and others – how we communicate (or maybe fail to), what drives us, and how various interactions impact us. We can call this psychologising or mentalising – or simply think of it as discovering what makes us tick, or 'figuring it out'.

The International Coach Federation considers that the following are essential features of professional supervision: that it

- provides an opportunity to better understand self, the client, the client's system and the choices made within the engagement;
- raises awareness of personal reactions to the client and/or the system and provides a safe place for exploring these;
- serves a restorative and iterative function.[9]

In 'Ways of looking, ways of seeing' (Chapter 2), we explore ways of seeing and ways of being with others. Our key framework is Transactional Analysis (TA), which we describe along with examples and illustrations from practice. We explore how beliefs and philosophies influence what each practitioner does, the range of how we choose to work and relate to our supervisees, including a description of some familiar and current models of supervision and a number of TA concepts – some widely known and others more recently developed.

A focus on context and task

However we understand what we are doing in supervision; the starting place is that there is a job to be done. We need to be aware of the potential power of what we do, and maintain an appropriate mind-set for our practice. Two chapters are useful here:

In 'Relational needs: the supervision triangle' (Chapter 3), we discuss what supervision is for, introducing a model that has become a cornerstone in our training along with an overview of what we are doing as supervisors, and how we balance out the essential tasks of supervision. The 'three functions of supervision' are well known, but this triangle model helps to illustrate the importance of keeping a balance between the three functions – providing a useful check for experienced supervisors as well as a guide for those who are just beginning.

In 'Creating effective contracts: empathy and rigour' (Chapter 5), we introduce another key concept: contracting is the basis of all good work – we build on this foundation to clarify how the supervisor recognises, understands and does what they are there for. We discuss how the contract varies between different contexts, and how empathy and rigour inform our approach. We also describe one-to-one, three-way and multiple contracts; levels of contracting (including the social, professional and psychological), ways of working with groups, and organisational contracts.

Reflective practice, relational style, narrative and storytelling

Supervision is a supreme opportunity for learning – by reflecting on lived experience. This 'reflective method' enhances mutual learning for supervisee and supervisor, and, at the same time, turns the work into a kind of action research where data and findings build into a continuing cycle through which everyone can grow and change. This approach is closely linked to the 'relational turn'[10] in adult learning: it seeks integration and meaning rather than pre-set answers or solutions. As we are all storytellers, a narrative way of thinking, linked to new ideas about life-scripts and how we can change them, opens up the prospect of fresh stories and insights.

We use stories a lot throughout this book, telling stories from our own experience and from that of our colleagues – and sometimes suggesting you join in with the story by asking how it might be different. At the end of some of the chapters, we relate longer stories to demonstrate something we have learnt about ourselves and our work.

In 'Learning in relationship' (Chapter 4), we investigate how learning happens in supervision; the theories that underpin our training and the connections between script theory, learning, relational and co-creative approaches.

An ethical attitude

The values that underpin and inform all that we do, that hold us all to account, are the reason why we want to do this work: why we are concerned to challenge, to bother grappling with the ethical concerns, to live with our inadequacies and frustrations, to confront fear and shame – and to find courage and compassion for ourselves and for others.

In 'Success and safety: the context and ethics of supervision' (Chapter 6) we define the territory, identify some of its potential minefields, and suggest ways of relating values, principles and practices, boundaries and responsibilities. This chapter covers the legal aspects of supervision, the 'mores', cultural differences in our ethical assumptions, and links these to insights from egostate and script theory.

Practical implications

What do supervisors actually do? In Chapter 7, we review methods of supervision; how our practice varies when we work one-to-one, with groups and teams, in organisations. A major part of this chapter is to consider the impact of topics discussed in the preceding chapters on working practice. There are sections on leading groups, methods for group supervision and the job of the supervisee.

And, a key point – a positive stance

In this book, and in our practice, we focus particularly on the supervision of coaches – whether they work with their clients in an organisational or a personal context.

However, our way of working lends itself to working with almost anyone who uses their coaching skills in business, schools and hospitals, therapy centres, etc. Our requirement is that supervisors should be continually aware of the one-to-one relationships (where the majority of the initial scrutiny will take place), the one-to-many relationships, and the broader social contexts in which they sit.

What you will find

Each chapter includes the theoretical base, together with an analysis – often from TA concepts and principles – and illustrations from real-life case studies to demonstrate the connection between approach, practice and outcome. Chapters are in the order that made sense to us, but you may want to read 'Learning in relationship' first to follow up on what we have said here about our view of supervision. Or again, you might prefer to go straight to Chapter 7 for some hands-on input. Whatever you choose, we have aimed to make connections between the chapters and to follow our key themes throughout.

At the beginning of each chapter, there is a mind-map of its content. At the end of each chapter, there are notes for those who want to follow up the ideas, plus some information about the sources we have drawn on. We have chosen to add these as notes rather than include academic references within the text – though we will sometimes do that when it seems important.

Overall, we want to create a 'story' of supervision: there is a specific location for supervision set in the landscape of the human relations field, especially coaching; and there are many characters in the story – including you and us in dialogue.

The story begins with a challenge: how can we find an understanding – create a unique vision – of what happens in supervision? All of us, supervisors, coaches, clients, join in exploring the meaning of the relational process and the complexity of personal-to-professional interactions. We will discover tools and skills that can bring resolution, new learning, encouragement to go on growing.

So, our invitation is to engage in an adventure, believing in the possibility of change, being fully present, honest, courageous – and to be vulnerable, to tolerate uncertainty, to be open to learning, to be excited and stimulated, seeking challenge and enjoying it – and to be in a relationship, working co-creatively together.

We write from our own perception, which we want to share with you, hoping it is something that we can all develop and grow together. It is grounded in our own experience, in the myriad influences and inspirations of our personal histories of doing and teaching supervision.

This book is a practical guide to doing supervision in the coaching world, together with reflections on supporting theories, but it is not a comprehensive overview of coaching supervision covering all current approaches; at the end, in Further Reading, we recommend some books that do this.

We do, however, want this book to be the basis of a forum for everyone interested in developing the profession and its competences; a body of practical thinking that can be added to, enhanced and updated, by us and others as the profession grows and develops.

At the end, you will find a reflective discussion of 'What next?' where we share our ideas and hopes about the future of coach supervision – and supervision in general – and repeat our invitation to you to engage in this discourse.

Notes

We say 'we' when we write about our own thinking and what we have learnt from our work, even though it may be just one of us writing – so you may notice different voices in this text.

Sometimes, for instance in stories about supervision, the 'we' becomes an 'I' – most often meaning one of us, but sometimes another supervisor who has shared a story with us.

The stories we tell are from our own supervision work or that of our colleagues. Some are amalgams of several situations we have encountered. We use them to illustrate and to trigger thinking. All contexts have been disguised and proper names changed.

Since we are writing about coach supervision, we use 'coach' and 'supervisee' for the person being supervised, according to context. 'Client' always means the coach's client – whether they are an individual or an organisation.

Notes

1 Thanks to Cesare Fregola for this idea.
2 The radical Brazilian educator, Paulo Freire, and his colleague, Mike Horton, chose the title, 'We make the road by walking' for their book published in 1991. It is a record of their conversations about the project of radical education and community development, and includes the passage – significant for us:

> I didn't want the expert to tell (the group) what to do. I wanted the expert to give them the facts and let them decide what to do. There's a big difference in giving information and telling people how to use it.
>
> (Horton & Freire 1991 p. 129)

3 Figures on supervision statistics are from www.business.brookes.ac.uk/.../coaching-supervision.../Eve-Turner-slides-5th-Int-Coaching..,.11 Jul 2015. Accessed 17 February 2017.
4 Many of the diagrams and ideas in the following chapters were first put forward in the manual *Supervision for Coaches: A guide to thoughtful work* and have since been revised, extended and generally tussled with between us and our colleagues.
5 The phrase, 'How we work is who we are' is taken from a keynote address delivered by Diana Shmukler, psychotherapist and professor of psychology, at a conference of IARTA in 2010. The full text can be found in *Relational Transactional Analysis: Principles in practice* (Fowlie & Sills 2011). We find it inspiring, and a concise summary of our approach. Although Diana was speaking as a therapist to therapists, we feel that the same premise can apply to supervision, and that this accounts for the therapeutic effect supervision often has.
6 Rilke, R. M., *Letters to a Young Poet,* p. 21.
7 Michael Carroll writes about spirituality and supervision in Chapter 6 of *Integrative Approaches to Supervision* (2001), suggesting similarities between supervision and spirituality – in sharing a shift from isolation and stasis to connectedness and development, and from individual to communal, through a process of continual reflection. He ends his chapter by quoting R. D. Laing, 'There is nothing to be afraid of'.
8 Carole Shadbolt and William Cornell discuss the 'terminology' of supervision or consultancy in a TAJ article which is part of a special issue on Supervision (Cornell & Shadbolt 2007).
9 Source for the characteristics of supervision is the ICF chart 'Differences between supervision, mentoring and coaching', Oct. 2015.
10 'Relational turn' – this expression is taken from Fowlie and Sills (2011).

Chapter 1

What is supervision?

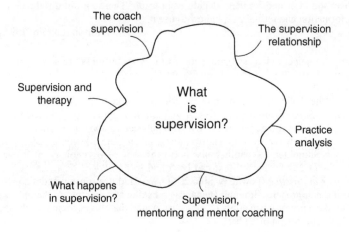

The coach supervision

The supervision relationship

Supervision and therapy

What is supervision?

Practice analysis

What happens in supervision?

Supervision, mentoring and mentor coaching

The start of a supervision session is like the opening of a show: you've looked at the programme and the house lights have gone down; the red velvet curtains draw back, but all you can see is a shallow strip of stage with another painted curtain behind it, a static image holding the possibility of something beyond it – but not the reality.

And, then, as the lights shine behind this curtain, you see that it is in fact a gauze – and revealed behind it are the players, the action, the full depth and perspective of the stage. Now we have something worth engaging with.

And this is how it is in supervision: we reveal what lies behind the static, two-dimensional image. This is our territory – this is where we want to explore.

The theatre metaphor describes an experience we willingly enter into, that contains layers of both illusion and reality. It will never, ever, be the same twice. What we see on the stage can't be repeated because both the characters and their audience are developing moment by moment. We are in a relationship where both parties are changed by their here-and-now experience.

Theatre is built on the creation of a version of reality but is in fact a mystery. When you pull back the curtains and turn on the bright white working lights you can see how all of that experience has been created by the technicians and the actors with wood and metal, nuts and bolts, rope and fabric, sound and light. It isn't mysterious any more; it all makes complete sense. You have moved from the limited perspective of the audience into a wider dimension of understanding – making sense of the experience and how it has been created.

Like our engagement with the theatre, once we've realised what's happening on the stage, in supervision we want to know how each of the elements of the story has come to be – the intention of the relationship, the interaction between client, coach, supervisor and the wider system – and to understand how we have created our own response to it.

And, yes, there are many elements here, and it will take a lot of work to understand them all. But at each stage in our exploration, more is revealed to enrich us and help us develop the way we want to work in the future. We begin to grasp what is easy for us, what we think we may never understand, the bits we love to get to grips with and those where we might rather have stayed with our illusions.

So, just like the theatre, things are revealed stage by stage – as we're ready.

We all grow best when we feel safe enough to be challenged, safe enough to be adventurous, safe enough to disclose and admit mistakes – when we're not afraid of exposure. We grow best where equality is present and power is available to each and appropriately deployed – where responsibility can be negotiated and promises made and held to. In such a relationship, what was opaque can become clear and what has been in the darkness can be enjoyed in the light.

The supervision relationship

Supervision essentially describes a relationship between two practitioners, both of whom are working in the field of professional personal development. When this relationship includes trust and mutual respect it enables each of the participants to have the courage to celebrate who they are and what they are proud of – and to confront and resolve those aspects that cause them to experience defensiveness, disappointment, shame, frustration and even grief.

This is not rescuing or befriending or comforting (all of which may sometimes show up in supervision) because this relationship is clearly contracted and re-contracted for throughout its lifetime. For it to truly work both parties need to be willing to be vulnerable – to not know, to be confused or lost – whilst on the journey to clarity and progress.

For each partner in the supervision relationship all of their learning flows from within that relationship. If 'how we work is who we are', then supervision needs to be about supervisor and supervisee jointly questioning the way in which 'who the supervisee is' is manifested in 'how they work'. And as we begin to develop 'how we work', 'who we are' will also grow.

This is how learning happens: all the thinking that has happened on our supervisor training courses has contributed to our recognition that supervision is 'learning in relationship'; a place to create an understanding that can be taken back into those other, workplace, relationships.

At its best, we think the supervision relationship is:

- a place of empathy and rigour; a place of possibility and safety, without personal judgement;
- a place where both partners can be truthful;
- a collegial relationship where there is authenticity, a balance of power, and both parties are absolutely accepted;
- a place where there is joy in learning and no fear of disclosure;
- a place where learning is noticed and recognised, and competence is brought into awareness.

This, then, is the real essence of 'how we work is who we are'.

The supervision relationship happens within a contract which combines rigour and empathy. This contract will be the 'container' for the relationship, defining its purpose and nature: what it is – and what it is not.

Without the rigour of a clear contract, how do we know what we are setting out to achieve – or if we have achieved it? How do we know whether we have an ethical dilemma or not? How can we be sure we are doing something truly and professionally valuable, as opposed to simply colluding when we meant to nurture, undermining when we meant to challenge, controlling when we meant to manage?

Without an empathic relationship, how can we create the conditions of trust and mutual understanding which both allow and enable real learning?

The key to the supervision relationship, and the work that is possible within it, is to create a robust balance between the 'container' (a clear and structured contract) and the 'content' (the empathic understanding and intuition which allow 'leaps of learning').

What happens in supervision?

Coaching has rapidly become established and recognised as a profession. Supervision, as an accepted part of that professionalisation process, is relatively new.

As the coaching world grows, so there is an increasing need for a body of well-trained, informed practitioners who understand the ethics, responsibilities, practices and defining features of this developing profession. Accountability to clients, organisations and the coaching profession is a major aspect of our view of coach supervision, creating an ongoing dialogue between the personal and the professional, the relationship and the responsibility.

Coaching supervision aims to locate when, how and why the personal (the coach's stuff) intrudes into the professional (the space in which coach and client are working). What does this reveal to both coach and supervisor about where change and growth need to occur in order to better serve the clients? It may well be that what happens between supervisor and coach also points to learning – so the relationship itself can be a vehicle for growth.

Mentoring and professionalisation

At first, the coach supervisor pool tended to be filled by coaches who had become senior in the coaching profession and felt they had the expertise (and the life experience and wisdom) to contribute to those following in their footsteps. This was most often described as 'mentoring' and was hugely helpful in bringing new coaches up to a professional standard of competence.

A less helpful element was that, in some cases, the mentoring relationship was based on a belief in expertise that had remained unchallenged and unmodified over the years. Unless the supervisor had had their own experience of being supervised, there was little examination of the coach's internal world and the impact of their own filters and experiences on the way in which they worked with their clients.

There may have been little awareness of using the supervisor's own internal experience as a 'lens' through which to gain understanding of what was going on in the various client relationships under observation.

About ten years ago, supervisors began to see their role as one of building a relationship of mutual challenge, vulnerability and development. They were now willing to be 'the one who is stronger and wiser in the moment', but they contained this within the humility to know that the other is truly the expert on themselves; they need to be supported in their growth but not told how to grow.

Supervision and motivation

Today, more coaches want to train professionally as supervisors and see it as a way of improving their own practice. There is also an emerging group of those who only want to be supervisors – and not work at all as coaches.

Supervisors are many and various: some would like to give something back; some to be actively engaged in the professionalisation of coaching; and some still want to be the custodians of 'what is right'. For some of us, it is about the joy of a truly collegial relationship and the chance to learn with and contribute to the learning of others who we like and admire as peers. And, sometimes, to see them overtake us and climb the next hill, waving at us to follow on behind!

Supervision is becoming the most effective way of sustaining the development of the client and the coach, the wider system in which they both operate, as well as the supervisor and the coaching profession. We are delighted that supervision, like coaching, is set to develop into a 'broad church' with a shared basis of sound ethics and values. We believe that supervision for coaches should model the practice of coaching itself, i.e. that it should share the same structures, be purposeful in the same way, be forward-moving and outcome-oriented, and ultimately demonstrable in visible behavioural change in the coach.

Models for understanding

There has been – and there still is – some debate about whether coaches need to have an underpinning psychological model in order to be effective. *The Sage Handbook of Coaching*,[1] for instance, includes thirteen psychological approaches and eleven 'genres' or contexts for coaching.

It may be that not all of these contexts demand 'minded-ness' from coaches (or their clients), but supervision does: to recognise the intrusions of the personal into the professional we need to have some kind of model to understand how and why this happens and what the risks and potential effects may be.

Learning how this can happen (and how to deal with it if it does) is the theme of the rest of this book. Whatever your chosen model may be for understanding 'what makes people tick' – hopefully a mixture of cognitive and psychodynamic insights – we want to share some perspectives and insights that we ourselves have gained, and offer them into the fusion of a developing philosophy of coach supervision.

To sum up, we think that coach supervision:

- is based in a contracted relationship;
- demonstrates 'how we work is who we are';
- models coaching practice in bringing about observable change;
- ensures accountability in the coaching profession;
- provides a safe space for exploration;
- is a place of mutual learning;
- combines structure (the contract) with empathy (rapport/connection).

And is at its core:

- a supreme learning experience for both supervisee and supervisor;
- action learning (and action research) connecting theory and practice;
- a growth process (as well as a regulatory system) with an impact on others, for instance commissioning organisations.

How is supervision different from other partnerships?

There are various supportive professional relationships which, without being supervision, can be invaluable for practitioners' development. An obvious one, which often elicits much discussion on supervisor training courses, is mentoring or 'mentor coaching'. Others include coaching itself, which could be, for instance, to enhance a coach's own business practice, or therapy and counselling on specific issues that lie beyond the scope of supervision. We will return to these below, but first we introduce another form of partnership in people work.

Practice analysis

An important distinction we have identified is between practice analysis[2] and other forms of supervision. The term comes from an adult education/training model which distinguishes it from supervision while acknowledging that both are necessary.

In practice analysis, the practitioner is helped to progressively build their own practice through a growing awareness and examination of the situations they encounter. They do this with the support of a facilitator – but without teaching, theory discussion or problem-solving techniques. This process often, but not necessarily, takes place in a group where there will be learning for the other group members as well.

The objective is to facilitate the management of difficulties through observation, reflection and the building of collective expertise. The aim is to get the practitioner to stand back and not become immersed in the problem, to better understand their own actions and the reasons for their success or failure:

> to identify the various components, to identify their intricacy, and to identify the implicit underlying acts and conduct in the situation as an object of study. This work of highlighting aims at an objectification, an understanding that makes it possible to distance and seek greater coherence in the practice of the work.[3]

This format is similar to the learning cycle approach discussed in Chapter 4. The person who is working describes a situation, their experience and perceptions, and what happened next. Then the exploration is widened by the whole group through questions and reflection. A new way of understanding the situation is reached and a course of future action decided upon by the person who brought the problem. This is, of course, what often happens in a supervision group. Practice analysis shares with supervision a reflective approach; both are valid and useful, but they are different.

Applying this to coaching: in practice analysis we look at 'what happened' in a particular context and how it relates to the particular competencies required for that profession; what that reveals about the strengths and gaps in the coach's capability; and the development of a plan for how additional skills development and practice is to be developed to improve the overall performance of the coach. In this way, practice analysis is poised somewhere between mentoring and supervision. Figure 1.1 makes this clear, showing the component parts of any piece of supervision.

In practice analysis, most of the time is spent on 'C', considered from various perspectives: the institution, its political and emotional resonance, and also the relationship between 'A' and 'C'. 'B' may be a mentor who stays 'alongside'. In supervision, the focus is on 'A' and 'A+B', including B's 'resonance' and any potential collusion or over-identification.

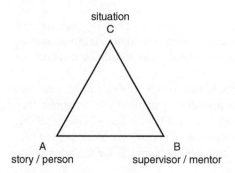

Figure 1.1   Practice analysis.

Practice analysis often happens within a supervision group, with learning for the whole group, but it can also become a part of individual supervision when there is a need to understand what went on at a systemic level.

For supervision (when the emphasis is on the personal) 'B' does not need to know too much about 'C'; but for practice analysis 'B' is expected to have appropriate professional knowledge and experience. 'B' will also need to be a good facilitator of the group's process and development as each member acquires their individual professional identity. Some supervisors are great at this – without necessarily being comfortable with other forms of supervision.

Practitioners in any kind of people-work, including coaches, need both supervision and practice analysis, though the balance may vary according to the individual's stage of development: new coaches may want more practice analysis to help them build their identity.

Again, 'A' may be resistant to revealing their personal experience in a group and want to take it into one-to-one supervision – even so, they will be learning in the group how to examine their own and others' practice. The idea is to hypothesise and discuss open questions rather than plan options, and the group can do this together.

Introducing a group of supervisors to the concept of practice analysis is sometimes a revelation, especially if they are supervising teams or projects.

> With a group of executive coaches, all of whom were working with teams within organisations, either as team coaches or as supervisors of internal coaches, we found that the recognition that it is possible, and beneficial, to distinguish the two approaches was liberating for everyone. They were able to stop asking themselves, 'Is this supervision?' and realise that practice analysis has its place.

As you read on, you may think we are not always completely clear about separating practice analysis and supervision. In a supervision session, it is true that both will occur at times. A handy guide is to ask, 'Is this about how to do something, or is it about why this keeps happening?'

Does it matter? Both are important – the one for professional development and improving how we work, the other for personal growth in a professional context and for the expansion of understanding, connectedness, compassion and mutuality.

In an effective supervision relationship there will be a balance, perhaps more of a dance, between considering practice and reflecting on what it means for the participants, both individually and in a group. To look at the two side by side sheds light on what can sometimes be a confusion around supervision. Previous understandings of supervision sometimes conveyed 'control', even if it wasn't overtly stated; and this may be part of a supervisee's anxiety or hesitation. Today, the focus has moved to ongoing support for learning about yourself in the work you do, whatever your field may be.

Supervision, mentoring and coaching

We have had many debates on training courses and elsewhere about the similarities and differences between supervision, mentoring and coaching. Table 1.1 shows the differences in terms of definitions, purpose, scope and focus; how the three are different in intention.[4]

Supervision, mentoring and coaching also differ in how they are delivered, perceived and experienced. Figure 1.2, created by a group of new supervisors on a training course, illustrates the overlaps and separate areas.[5]

We consider the sections of the diagram in turn, their individual characteristics, and what they have in common:

1   Supervision involves identifying, naming, and working with parallel processes; being in a learning partnership; holding the focus on the coach's client work. It requires awareness of multiple perspectives, including a meta-perspective of the system. The supervisor will be taking some responsibility for the work of the coach-supervisee, so their own agenda will be relevant and present. They will be 'wiser' in the moment, maintaining an

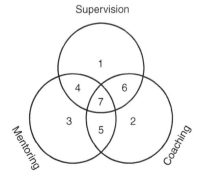

Figure 1.2   Supervision, mentor coaching and coaching: differences and similarities.

Table 1.1 Comparing mentoring, supervision and coaching

	MENTOR COACHING	COACHING SUPERVISION	COACHING
DEFINITION	... provides professional assistance in achieving and demonstrating the levels of coaching competency demanded by the desired credential level sought by a coach-applicant (mentee);	... is a collaborative learning practice to continually build the capacity of the coach through reflective dialogue and to benefit their clients and the overall system;	... is partnering with clients in a thought-provoking and creative process that inspires them to maximise their personal and professional potential.
PURPOSE	to reach or maintain a particular standard, or demonstrate specific coaching competencies and other credentialing requirements;	to co-generate insights through guided reflective enquiry that will improve the quality of their coaching – and hence expand the coach's capacity, capability, and confidence;	to increase the client's effectiveness, build relationships and reach their goals.
SCOPE	typically associated with a specific step in the coach's development, such as gaining a credential;	typically accessed throughout a coach's professional lifetime in terms of 'clean and clear' practice and continual growth as a coach;	as contracted with client/sponsor/ organization
FOCUS	specific to skill and competency building and maintenance;	broad ranging, including every aspect of the coach's self that may contribute to or hinder them as a coach;	broad ranging, but bound by the scope of coaching rather than any other professional approaches.

Adapted from 'Differences between supervision, mentoring and coaching', ICF 2015.

emphasis on questions and interventions, extra accountability, together with an awareness of legalities and ethics.
2   Coaching mostly involves keeping the coach's own agenda aside: a client focus; asking, not telling; support for the client's own development rather than for the greater system
3   Mentor coaching involves expertise; modeling and tutoring. It involves a transfer of skill, knowledge or technique.

In the overlaps:

4   Both mentor coaching and supervision involve appropriate 'telling' of experience; the use of specific methodologies for multiple parties, e.g. their organisation as well as the individual participants.
5   Both mentor coaching and coaching involve an appropriate competency level for their purpose; the modelling of competencies in their approach to the work in hand; building capability and resource in the coach/client; a responsibility for coach/client development rather than for the greater system.
6   Both supervision and coaching involve self-awareness: voicing one's own experience; believing that the client is whole and resourceful; respecting difference and collegiality; being willing to go with intuitive feelings or hunches.
7   All three involve a focus on development: valuing equal power in the relationship, feedback, mutual and self-respect, acceptance; observations and noticings, momentum, reflection, co-creation; offering a professional service (including getting paid) with a focus on what will now be practically different.

One member of the group that created this diagram shared his experience of working with a different professional for each of his needs:

> As he is moving towards semi-retirement, he talks with his coach about the changes he is making in his working patterns, the changes he aims to make in future and how these are currently impacting him.
>
> He has many hours of coaching behind him, but has never sought accreditation for that level. Through being coached, he has realized that he wants to make that step as much to acknowledge to himself what he has done and achieved as for professional status. So he now also works with a mentor coach to prepare for assessment.
>
> And, alongside both of these, he has regular supervision to which he brings any current concerns about specific clients or the organisations he contracts with, as well as the patterns that he senses in his work.

Each relationship is distinct, but all of them are part of his professional commitment and his growth in his chosen role.

What happens within supervision?

Figure 1.3 shows some of the ways of relating that may be part of supervision.[6]
This continuum gives a developmental picture of ongoing supervision as it moves its focus from management ('intervene', 'assess') to support ('facilitate', 'co-work'). The roles and activities the supervisor might employ are shown along the left side of the line, the consequent actions and processes to the right.

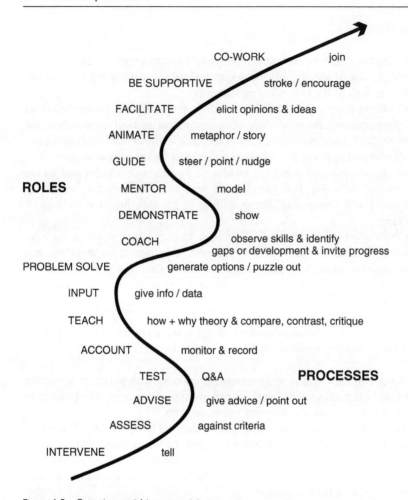

CO-WORK   join

BE SUPPORTIVE   stroke / encourage

FACILITATE   elicit opinions & ideas

ANIMATE   metaphor / story

GUIDE   steer / point / nudge

ROLES   MENTOR   model

DEMONSTRATE   show

COACH   observe skills & identify
gaps or development & invite progress

PROBLEM SOLVE   generate options / puzzle out

INPUT   give info / data

TEACH   how + why theory & compare, contrast, critique

ACCOUNT   monitor & record

TEST   Q&A   **PROCESSES**

ADVISE   give advice / point out

ASSESS   against criteria

INTERVENE   tell

Figure 1.3   Functions within supervision.

Source: Adapted from Newton and Napper 2007, p. 151.

In supervision with a relatively inexperienced coach, the focus may be at the lower end of the line – and have much in common with mentoring or practice analysis. As the coach grows and matures into autonomy the work becomes more collegial.

All these tasks and activities are possible ingredients in the rich blend that supervisor and supervisee will create together.

What is a coach supervisor?

Supervision is not about 'coaching coaches', nor is it about 'coaching the client through the coach'. It is about working with the coach in their own space. In this way, we can develop a more polished and professional expertise, secure in the knowledge that we are working ethically and providing security for both coach and client.

We believe that supervision is the most important element in continuing coach development. Once the coach has engaged in training and is gaining experience with clients, supervision will accelerate their competence, maintain professional and ethical standards and protect the psychological health of the coach. It will also be a major contributor in ensuring a positive and useful experience for their clients.

When we began delivering coach supervisor training and interviewing possible participants, we realised that many superb coaches are not natural supervisors – some course members found it hard to move from their coaching role to take on the meta-perspective, the evaluative function necessary for a supervisor.

In practical terms, how could we enable coaches in making this transition? Our way was to encourage trainee coach supervisors to think what they wanted and expected of an effective supervision relationship for themselves as supervisees and beginning supervisors.

We asked them to reflect on these questions – you might like to ask them of yourself:

- What, for you, are the attributes of an effective supervisor?
- How will you know when you are being effective?
- What do you think you need to learn in order to make that happen?
- What are you already doing to develop yourself into an effective supervisor?
- How has that been useful and how did you contribute to that usefulness?
- What was not useful and what have you learnt from that?
- What do you notice about yourself as a supervisor?
- What beliefs, assumptions, personal issues have been stirred up for you by this process?

This exercise produced some thought-provoking responses: an effective supervisor is someone who

- can inspire others;
- knows themselves quite well – and still likes themselves;
- will stay present while enjoying the collegial space;
- enjoys others' learning, while owning their own opinions and experience;
- is conscious of power relationships and has their own responses in the process, using the self as an instrument – and so is willing both to be vulnerable and to step into a place of authority when needed;
- will self-challenge to explore what they do;
- will develop over time to become a more sophisticated practitioner.

This adds up to a supervisor who continues to learn and grow and who is willing to stay in the place of 'conscious competence' (which Petruska Clarkson called 'The Master') – staying aware of how they are being and working; not risking the 'unconscious competence' of mechanically assuming that everything is accounted for without checking – and thus falling into 'unconscious incompetence'.[7]

You might be thinking that all these qualities are also desirable for mentors and coaches – and of course we agree. However, we believe that for supervisors there are some add-ons: they can be recognised in the above responses. Good supervisors may use their coaching and/or mentoring skills in the moment, but these will always be backed by an awareness of the meta-perspective; by taking account of more than the coach's own perceptions.

Together with our colleagues we have identified the characteristics and attitudes likely to make someone a valuable and successful supervisor.

An effective supervisor will

- have life and work experience, and have been active as coach since coach training (2–3 years' experience is a minimum);
- be interested in the development of others, and enjoy others' learning;
- be interested in the development of coaching;
- have the ability to stand in another's shoes, to take a broad perspective;
- be willing to operate in an open and equal learning environment;
- be willing to own their experience and opinions;
- be willing to step into a place of authority when needed;
- be able to trust themselves;
- have clarity of purpose in being a supervisor;
- be willing to use their own experience in the moment and to be reflective;
- be able to differentiate what is ethical, professional and useful in their own reactions;
- stay in a respectful yet autonomous position;
- enjoy the collegial space;
- be up for self-challenge;
- be conscious of potential imbalances of power in their supervision relationships.

The required competencies for coach supervisors are still being debated in the various coaching associations. In 'Competencies for coach supervision' you will find a list that integrates the results of several years of discussion with course participants and relates competencies to the supervision triangle in Chapter 3 and the supervision checklist in Chapters 5 and 7.

Supervision or therapy

Supervision may be a truly therapeutic experience, in the sense of being beneficial, restorative and even curative; but it is not 'therapy' as understood within psychotherapy.

Some coaches may be in need of both supervision and therapy; part of the job of the supervisor is to detect when an issue, very powerfully felt or recurring in sessions time after time, indicates the need for a different kind of intervention.

This story illustrates just such a situation:

When I began working with my supervisor I had already done a great deal of personal development work.

However, in supervision it became increasingly clear that 'the personal was intruding into the professional'. When this happened I was 'ambushed' by emotions that usually expressed themselves as weepiness.

My supervisor and I discussed this, gaining some insights into what was happening with my client or their wider system to trigger this response; but it still felt as if there were things we weren't addressing, and that I personally couldn't access.

We danced around a number of options: did I actually need a spiritual director or was there old, childhood stuff that needed to be resolved by working with a therapist?

We went back and forth about this for almost two years. My supervisor would give me contacts which I didn't follow up; I looked on the web for therapists, and found one living close to my home, but didn't do anything about that either.

After a while of this, my supervisor said to me, 'Enough! Either you do something about this, or we need to stop talking about it. We both know this is limiting your development as a person and a professional; I have no idea why you are so resistant; you need to work this out for yourself – or overcome your resistance and find someone you trust and work it out with them.'

Because I knew my supervisor cared deeply about me and my development, I realised she was fulfilling our contract. She was willing to be direct: to confront me in such a way that it was clear I could no longer just rely on her supporting me. She was willing to challenge me and, yes, manage me … and take responsibility for telling me what I needed to hear.

In that moment with her, I finally confronted my deep-seated fear of looking into my own past. I decided to find a therapist, and my supervisor helped me to clarify what my criteria would be: she insisted that I interview at least two … and I was very glad she did: I briefly talked through both interviews with her and came to a solid decision.

And it was a great decision. My therapist and I have worked together well. I have confronted my deepest fears, and brought what was obscure into the light of the here and now. As the 'grown-up me', I've come to terms with what I have found. As a coach and a supervisor the process has helped me enormously.

I am rarely 'ambushed' by my emotions now; I'm pretty good at distinguishing – in the moment with a client or afterwards in supervision – between my stuff and theirs. And, personally, I am much happier.

But the key to all of this was my supervisor, who was willing to step up to her responsibilities to me as her supervisee.

Notes

1   Cox, E., Bachkirova, T. and Clutterbuck, D., eds *The Complete Handbook of Coaching* (2nd edition) (London: Sage 2014).
2   Thanks to Evelyne Papaux for inspiration and information on how practice analysis contributes to the range of supervision activities.
3   Papaux, E. personal communication (course notes).
4   Definitions etc. in the section on mentoring, coaching and supervision are adapted from the ICF comparison chart 'Differences between supervision, mentoring and coaching', October 2015. Many thanks to Pat Marum to making these available to us.
5   The Venn diagram and associated notes were developed on supervisor training courses between 2008 and 2011 – thanks to all participants for their input.
6   The diagram of 'Functions within supervision', was first published in the *Transactional Analysis Journal* article, 'The Bigger Picture' (Newton & Napper 2007).
7   In *The Achilles Syndrome* (1994, p. 55) Clarkson discusses the well-known model of experiential learning and adds her own names for the stages: unconscious incompetence, 'the fool'; conscious incompetence, 'the apprentice'; conscious competence, 'the master'; and unconscious competence, 'the mechanic'. She labels the terms this way to emphasise that we need to stay aware of our practice – so the master is the conscious practitioner, not the potentially mechanical unconsciously competent person who may take insufficient care to account for all aspects of the work.

Chapter 2

Ways of looking, ways of seeing

Perspectives on supervision

```
                                      Egostates
                     Assessment
                                          Transactional analysis
                                            Frame of reference
                                              Strokes
   Organisations         Ways of looking,
                         ways of seeing:      Cycles and stages
   PAC      Imagos       Perspectives on
                          supervision

         Making                    Parallel process
         contact
                             8-eyed model
                            Convergent process
```

I have learned most in supervision from the gift of generosity – a generous spirit.[1]

When you supervise, or are being supervised, do you have a 'framework' that you consciously work to – or do you go by intuition? Think for a moment about how you supervise. You may discover that you have a model or method so deeply integrated that it has become unconscious.

Imagine you are talking about this with a colleague. Tell them what idea or framework you started out with:

- What have you added to that, and why?
- What have you jettisoned, and why?
- How would you describe your framework now?
- How do you picture yourself as a supervisor?

A key component of effective supervision is our willingness to engage with new frameworks, to investigate them 'in the round' with our supervisees, jointly applying them to develop new understandings. There are many different ways of looking at what's going on for supervisor and supervisee in the work of supervision, and that 'looking' is highly influenced by so many things – our beliefs and values, our ethical frameworks, the environment, our current skill and capability, the behavioural norms with which we are familiar, the culture in which we are operating. It's important to consider how all these may impact outcomes. Without them we'd never get through a day in one piece; but as supervisors we need to be aware of them, and challenge them from a number of different perspectives.

In Chapter 7, we will concentrate on what happens moment by moment in supervision – the methods we use in real time; but now we want to explore the models and internal frameworks that inform our work: how we think about what we do, why we plan our route this way, and what signposts we find as we go.

> If coaching is about listening, supervision is perhaps more about seeing. It is also sometimes about speaking plainly, naming the danger or opportunity that lies on the path and suggesting, as a companion on the way, what the coach might do about this.
>
> It follows that a good supervisor is someone who can hold a position from where they can see clearly, who can dance between 'the coach' and 'what is happening in the coach's work', without being pulled so close to either that they lose a clear sense of both, and who can offer direction when needed.
>
> Most of the dangers in supervision – whether collusion or a tendency to instruct – come from the supervisor being pulled out of position or off balance, and failing to maintain the intuitive support and clear-sighted rigour essential to their work.[2]

Frame of reference and culture

We all have our own individual way of seeing the world, our 'frame of reference'.[3] It integrates the totality of our experiences, beliefs and expectations. It determines what we see, how we see it – and also what we fail to recognise. It is, inevitably, shaped by the culture we grow up in, by our family and social environment, by all the circumstances that impact us from childhood up to the present day.

Our frame of reference influences our perception, the meaning we give to whatever happens to us; it will also have an unconscious impact on what we think, feel and do. We can see this in action at those times when we feel at a loss to get alongside a colleague, a friend or a supervisee, or when observing some political discussions, or seeing delegates from very different cultures discussing how to implement a decision – nothing is going to change unless one or all of us shifts our frame. The good news is that frames of reference can be updated, adjusted, expanded: that's what happens in learning; we change our personal frame of reference, and sometimes even transform it.

What happens as we acquire our frame of reference? To explain, we will introduce transactional analysis and explore some of the ideas that inform our thinking and practice. This introduction is necessarily brief – you can find suggestions for more detailed reading in the notes for this chapter and there are further references in the bibliography.

Transactional analysis

Transactional Analysis[4] ('TA') began in the early 1960s, when Eric Berne set out to create a psychology that could be easily understood and which emphasised the mutuality between practitioner and client. From the beginning, he used diagrams to explain the concepts, expressing them in simple, everyday language.

TA is, first and foremost, a philosophy about how people can relate to themselves, others and the world; a philosophy colloquially summarised as 'I'm OK, you're OK'. In this apparently simple statement, we find an awareness of being in the world with others as independent but connected human beings (I am, you are), and a belief in trust and respect for each other and ourselves.

TA informs our supervision practice through a valuable thinking framework and an accessible language that can lead to a greater understanding of the motivations, interactions and outcomes experienced in the coaching conversation.

TA has three straightforward key principles that derive from its value base:

- A belief in the worth and dignity of all people, in mutual and self-respect; the acceptance of self and others: everyone is OK (I'm OK, You're OK and They're OK).
- A belief that everyone can think, and therefore find solutions to solve problems.
- A belief that anyone can change their behaviour, thinking or feeling (if and when they choose to).

Open communication and a contractual process is essential to TA practice: presenting people with the opportunity to change, while respecting their decision about how and when they want to do so.

Strokes and stages

Going back to how we develop our frame of reference, we all need to know that we 'matter' – that other people see us, recognise us, and understand what is important to us.

Recognition is known in TA as 'strokes', because we first experience them when we are small through touch. They enhance our self-esteem and self-identity and enable us to get on with the people around us – whether partners, family and friends, colleagues or clients – anybody we encounter as we go about the world.

A secure relationship in infancy generates endorphins which build the medial prefrontal cortex (the 'social brain'), and through repeated positive experiences synapses are established that enable us to expect positive interactions with others.[5]

As adults, we still benefit most from positive strokes that show that someone cares about us in some way ('I like you', 'Good work!'). If these are not forthcoming,

Table 2.1 Stages of development summary chart

	STAGES	TASKS OF CHILD	NEEDS, STROKES	HELPFUL BEHAVIOURS, KEY AFFIRMATIONS
1	Being 0–6m	Learn to get needs met; learn to trust; bond emotionally; accept care, touch.	Love, care, touch; consistency; you belong here; think for baby.	Consistent care; use touch, holding, talking, singing; be reliable; think for child as needed; 'You belong here'.
2	Doing 6–18m	Explore and experience; develop senses, initiative; learn to get help; form secure attachment.	Safety, encouragement, variety, protection, support; don't interrupt; OK to be active, quiet.	Provide encouragement, safe environment with varied sensory experiences; listen to child; respond and model language; 'You can do things as many times as you need to'.
3	Thinking 1½–3yrs	Learn to think, test reality, solve problems, express feelings; begin to separate; give up being centre.	Encourage thinking; give reasons, how-to's; accept feelings; set limits.	Give clear directions, information; stroke thinking; accept feelings; be consistent; 'You can think for yourself'.
4	Identity 3–6yrs	Assert separate identity; acquire info about self, place in family; test power; social behaviour; separate fantasy/reality.	Both sexes are OK; give info; answer questions; stroke OK behaviour; get own support.	Answer questions accurately; connect feeling and thinking; be clear about responsibilities; teach acceptance; 'You can explore who you are'.
5	Skills 6–12yrs	Learn skills; make mistakes; listen; reason; rules and structure in and out of family; values; disagree; test ideas; co-operate.	Lots of strokes; be reliable, clear; set rules; offer tools; allow consequences; challenge behaviour.	Teach conflict resolution, problem-solving; support skills development; respect child's opinions; 'You can find ways of doing things that work for you'.
6	Integration 12–18yrs	Separate; be independent, responsible; have own needs, values; integrate sexuality.	Understand, encourage, accept, support, discuss, celebrate.	Offer support; confront destructive behaviour; encourage independence; negotiate rules and responsibilities; 'You can be independent and develop your own interests and causes'.

Adapted from Barrow, Bradshaw and Newton 2001, p. 92.

we settle for negative strokes ('You messed up didn't you?', 'Get out!') – at least they mean another person has noticed us, even if we feel angry, hurt or depressed as a result!

We each have our individual expectations of what strokes we will receive, based mainly on what we discovered as we grew up about how the 'big people' (parents, teachers, older siblings) thought of us. These expectations become part of our frame. Some are good and life-enhancing, some not so good, limiting us and our development.

We pass through different stages as we grow from infancy to adulthood. In each stage, there are things we need to achieve (developmental tasks) and things we need from others to help us do so (strokes and affirmations). Table 2.1 shows these stages; what we learn as we experience them; what supports us in successfully completing each stage and moving on towards maturity.

Cycles of development[6]

The really good news is that we can – and do – revisit these stages later on (this is known as 'recycling'). We have a chance to find how to get the things that we missed out on, for whatever reason, the first time around. Figure 2.1, together with Table 2.1, illustrates how this works.

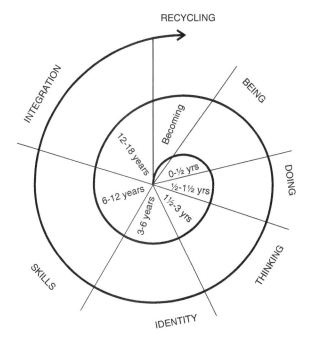

Figure 2.1   Cycles of development.

Source: Adapted from Levin-Landheer 1982, p. 136.

A fun thing to do – though not to be taken too seriously because there are often other factors to allow for – is to divide your actual age by twelve, take the remainder, and see if that corresponds to a stage on the cycle that feels appropriate for you right now.

> Soon after I took an important exam, not long before my sixtieth birthday, I became very passive, craving foods I don't normally eat (like French toast) and not wanting to make decisions. I had an excuse: I'd worked hard and needed a break, but that didn't feel like the reason.
>
> Once I realised I was going into a new 'Being' stage (60/12=5 and remainder is zero), I was able to give myself permission to enjoy it – but not stay there too long!

Another example of recycling is someone who struggles to achieve whenever they have to acquire new skills because they were taught in school or family to do things 'the right way' and never had permission to explore options for themselves. When offered straight and authentically, the affirmation from stage 5, 'You can find a way of doing things that works for you', can bring about almost miraculous change.

Egostates – ways of being

As we grow up and develop our individual view of the world, one of the things that we do is to 'file' our experiences into various categories in our mind: some as 'social responsibility' – how to behave towards other people; others as our individual objective 'take' on what is happening around us and what it means; yet others as our personal identity – 'This is what I myself feel, want and need.'

As shown in Figure 2.2, these three categories form our internal psychological structure or egostates, also known as 'P-A-C' (Parent, Adult, Child). We create the essential content in childhood, and we continue to draw on it as we grow into adulthood.

And, just as there are these three categories of 'content', so there are three corresponding categories of 'functioning'. These pictures of how we act in relation to others, our interactions and ways of communicating, our 'modes of behaviour', can be positive or negative – the latter may result from a lack of learning or of an awareness of strategies and options.[7]

So, in Parent we might positively structure or negatively criticise; supportively nurture or overprotect (Marshmallow); in Adult, account for all factors, in Child, we might be cooperating with others or resisting them, being creative and spontaneous or childishly immature. The preferred aim is to respond appropriately from a positive mode whatever the circumstances. All these elements can be seen in Figure 2.2.

Our Adult is continually taking in new information, responding and developing (when not limited by Parent beliefs or Child needs). In fact, we can 'update' all

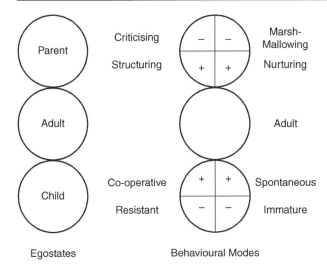

Figure 2.2   Egostates and functions.

our egostates to maximise the positive qualities: values and potency in the Parent, empathy and responsibility in the Adult, freedom and security in the Child.

Integrating Adult

Ideally, we can keep our internal Adult in charge as we interact with others and determine the most appropriate response to a situation. This may be caring, assertive, cooperative, joyful and so on – taking account of the context, our own needs and other people's, the professional and psychological contracts. This aspect of the Adult; integrating everything that is pertinent to the current circumstance, responding, looking for ways to account, constantly alert and seeking action/ expansion, has become known as the 'Integrating Adult'.[8]

Figure 2.3 shows how this works. The internal, integrating Adult makes decisions and choices about the most fitting way to move things on, using any or all of the positive modes of behaviour. Expanding the Adult is the desired aim – both for ourselves and for others.

The context is key: we can inhabit a variety of roles in different areas of our lives – our private world, our professional or organisational worlds, our community.[9] Sometimes, roles from one context may 'leak' into another – for example taking a 'parental' stance in a professional situation or a 'boss' role at home in the family. A supervisor might treat their supervision group the way they treat their adolescent children, perhaps too protectively, or not wanting them to be 'grown up'; after a frustrating week at work, an executive might find it hard to drop their demanding attitudes towards subordinates when they're at home – and initiate a row about the washing-up.

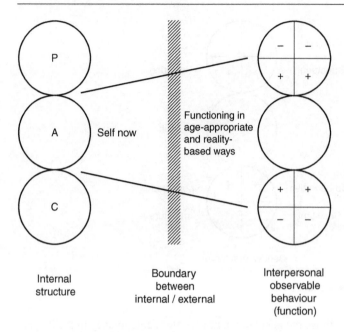

Figure 2.3   Relating structure and function.

Source: Napper and Newton 2014, 4:16.

Transactional analysis explores our observable interactions and the modes of behaviour we derive from our egostates. By monitoring and diagnosing our interactions we have a great resource to tell us how we see ourselves and others, how they might see us, how we 'block' or sabotage our own intentions, and how we could transact differently in order to get a different result.

Triangles of interaction

Just as we develop our own egostates when we are young, in response to whatever situation we find ourselves in, so we also establish our familiar ways of relating to others as we grow up and begin to extend our social contacts through family, school etc. This happens as we move through the Thinking and Identity stages in Table 2.1. As children, all of us are recipients of care and attention, instruction and guidance – and, of course, we are the centres of our own worlds.

As we grow, we learn to give help to others – siblings and parents at first – and to lead or show the way to others. We decide who we are, and what it means to be 'hero in our own story'. This is a healthy, normal process of growing and learning, shown as in Figure 2.4, and known as the triangle of social roles.[10]

We can move around the triangle, learning to give and take, to share tasks and take our turn. But – if good care and guidance is not modelled for us – we may learn ineffective or distorted ways of interacting with others. If continued into

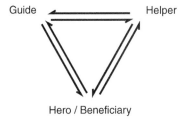

Guide — Helper

Hero / Beneficiary

Figure 2.4   The triangle of social roles.
Source: Le Guernic 2004, p. 220.

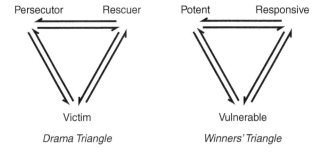

Persecutor   Rescuer   Potent   Responsive

Victim   Vulnerable

Drama Triangle   *Winners' Triangle*

Figure 2.5   The drama and winners triangles.
Source: Napper and Newton 2014, 9:6, 9.

adulthood, these can lead to relationships that limit us, as well as our partners and colleagues.

One of the most useful ways of exploring this is to become aware of what is possibly the single most useful TA model for the actual process of supervising: the drama triangle, along with its roles of Persecutor, Rescuer and Victim (Figure 2.5). This is an elegant way of mapping the positions we take in 'psychological game-playing' as we act out a distortion of the basic positions of 'guide', 'helper' or 'beneficiary'.

In transactional analysis, the term 'game' describes what happens when we engage in ineffective interactions that follow old, familiar patterns leading to negative outcomes. All of us sometimes get into games – attempts to make contact that go wrong. This happens when we feel in need of strokes (recognition) and 'play' from our preferred positions of helplessness (Victim), over-helpfulness (Rescuer) or harassment (Persecutor). As we play out our unconscious personal take on the relationship, we transact in familiar ways as we 'see' others in specific complementary roles.[11] When we get into game-playing we are also discounting: we ignore, minimise or belittle some aspect of the situation, or some part of ourselves or other people. Discounting means we are not accounting for something important or significant in solving the problem, whatever it might be. All psycho-logical games involve discounts.

The way to move from game-playing to authenticity is to recognise the truth behind the game roles – that people do sometimes have real problems which they haven't yet learnt the strategies to solve; are genuinely and appropriately concerned about others' welfare and can offer support without taking over; and can be asser-tive about what they can and can't do, without 'punishing' or blaming others.

The winners' triangle takes this 'OK' aspect of the roles and shows how we can act appropriately to restore mutual respect and good communication; how we can allow ourselves to be vulnerable, or offer responsive help, or proactively set boundaries.

With both supervisees and groups, the winners' triangle can be a very useful way to step away from games, but we have found that introducing the social roles triangle (Figure 2.4) goes even further in enabling people to normalise their expe-rience and understand the source of their distress.

Parallel process

In a training room, we asked students to take the roles of a coaching client, a coach, a first supervisor and a second supervisor. Both 'supervisors' then left the room. Everyone else stayed to observe.

We started with the 'client' bringing an issue to the coach; they engaged in a twenty-minute coaching session. At the end of this, the first supervi-sor came into the room to supervise the coach on the work they had just completed. When that session finished, the second supervisor came in and supervised the first supervisor on the work they had just done with the coach.

Amazingly, the key issue that emerged for the first supervisor was the same as the key issue for the coach – which was the same as the key issue for the original client. And remember, neither first nor second supervisor had been in the room for the previous work.

We have observed this outcome many, many times! So, what is going on here? When working with a coach as a supervisor, you may experience a rather odd feeling: possibly a sense of discomfort or anxiety – even a physical sensation such as a stiff neck or a tight chest. You may say to yourself that, 'This doesn't feel like me'. Chances are – it isn't!

A curious thing happens when we really open ourselves to the experience of another person – we start to 'echo' that experience ourselves. As a supervisor, you may find that you pick up your supervisee's experiences, feelings and behav-iours. And, oddly enough, what they are experiencing may not be theirs either – it could be derived from their clients, who may in turn be carrying something which is part of their wider organisational system. This has become known as 'parallel process'.

Very often, what shows up in supervision is a 'negative parallel process' – one that is unhealthy for anyone in the system. In supervision we can turn this round into a positive parallel process and 'send' that positive construct back down the line of people, out into the wider system.

In the 1950s, this experience was described as the 'reflection process' ('reflection' in this case means mirroring rather than thinking through). It was realised that the supervisor's experience, which had previously been thought of as either detached or involving their own unconscious need, could in fact be related to some area of difficulty in their supervisee's experience – or even to that of the supervisee's client:

> the processes at work currently in the relationship between [client] and [coach] are often reflected in the relationship between [coach] and supervisor.
>
> (Searles, our adaptation)[12]

We can learn to recognise when this is happening and check with the coach if it is relevant to their own or their client's situation. Alternatively, we can note it internally to inform our own questions and interventions.

Some questions for reflection:

- Do you notice similar patterns in what the supervisee brings every time? Do all of the supervisee's clients seem to have the same issue, to get stuck in the same way?
- Do you get a sense of, 'Here we go again!' or, 'Why do we always do this?'
- Do you notice that you are less able to access a particular area with this supervisee; be it management, support or challenge (Figure 3.1)?
- Are there things you realise you are not saying? Are you limiting your questions or challenges to the supervisee? Is the supervisee doing the same with their client? Is the client also behaving in this way in their relationships?
- Do you sense that the supervisee is not saying something they could say? Are you yourself holding something back?
- How long does it go on before something changes? Are you feeling that perhaps one or more of you are 'on' the drama triangle?
- Are there any other ways in which your interactions might be paralleling interactions that the supervisee and/or their client has with others – or that you have with others?
- Can you create a different frame or process that could be helpful in moving to a more constructive set of responses and actions?

By now you may have noticed that when we talk about 'parallel process' we are also talking about psychological games, or at least invitations to engage in games. The drama triangle is a highly effective way of looking at what may be happening; the winners' triangle is a good way of changing the parallel into a positive; and, finally, the social roles triangle enables us to focus on the underlying intention or need.

Parallel process offers a powerful narrative in supervision. Themes can pass both ways, from supervision to coaching as well as from coaching to supervision.

The process can be beneficial, as when the supervisor models 'positive parallel process' by being responsive rather than Rescuing, or by acting as guide rather than Persecutor – to the benefit of both supervisee and client.

The next two sections show ways of representing parallel process in action. Both are valuable in looking at the interactions between the supervision, the coach-client relationship and the wider context:

The eight-eyed model

Hawkins and Shohet's seven-eyed model[13] helps us map 'the whole territory': the context, the client, the coach and supervisor standpoints – and the potential parallels between them. We add an eighth layer – the ethos, the values and experience of those engaged in the work (Figure 2.6).

This way of mapping makes any parallel process visible; it is invaluable for gaining an overview of a supervision situation and for bringing to light an organisation's culture and frame of reference.

1   The Client System: The focus is on the client's situation; what they are bringing to the coaching, how they present the circumstances, both 'the raw data' and the choices that they are making.
2   The Coach's Interventions: The focus is on the strategies the coach used and the interventions they made; how and why they chose their strategy, how they chose to intervene – and what else they might have done.
3   The Relationship between Coach and Client: The focus is on the dynamic between the two: how does it relate to the system, what is the 'chemistry', how does the client experience the coach, and the coach the client? This will all be filtered through the coach's own perception of the client: what are they telling, what are they not telling?
4   The Coach: The focus is on the coach's own experience; how is the coach (unconsciously) affected in the process, what is being stimulated or

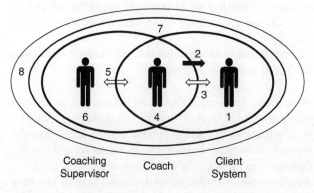

Figure 2.6   The eight-eyed model of supervision.

re-stimulated in them, what are they picking up? What resources does the coach have – and are they being used? What other resources do they need?

5   The supervisory relationship: The focus is on the quality of the relationship between coach and supervisor – what is being played out in the here-and-now; the positive and negative parallel process.

6   The supervisor's own process: The focus is the supervisor's current inner experience; is this 'imported' from (or via) the coach? What light does this shed on the coach-client relationship? The supervisor is aware of shifts and changes within themselves and what these might mean.

7   The Wider Context: The focus is on the wider organisational context: are there conflicts of interest, ethical or organisational issues; is something being avoided … because ….?

8   And, yes, there's an eighth 'eye': The contact, awareness, connectedness, overall values and philosophy that the supervisor is bringing into the process, beneficial to the wider context as well as all the other participants. When this is in good shape it will affect the supervision relationship constructively, whatever issues or concerns are brought.

This model is a robust and useful tool; it is an extremely useful way of analysing – and revealing new truths about – what has been brought to supervision.

As a practice, if the group – peer or training – is large enough, one of the participants can stand (literally, spatially) in the position of each 'eye'.

What about the client?

I used this with a group, all of whom were up for giving it a go. They were all confident, well-trained, and had reasonable relationships with each other.

We contracted for our roles and our boundaries, and all went well in the early stages: the 'client' was at the centre, the 'coach' described the work and the dilemma to the 'supervisor', and each of the 'eyes' watched and listened.

Then, eye by eye, we 'unpacked' what we had seen and heard, the meanings we were making and the emotions we were experiencing. We also unpacked what each of our learnings had been.

We were feeling quite satisfied – and then the 'client' burst into tears.

She had felt utterly discounted in the work. Yes, we'd all been respectful in our language, we'd not judged her challenges in any way, we'd held her to be OK and a great data provider … but we hadn't acknowledged her humanity. And, crucially, we hadn't acknowledged that without her we would have had no work! She was the centre, the heart, the giver of the existential energy, which enabled our whole system to be effective!

I learnt a lesson that day that I've never forgotten: the end-client – the coach's client – is the energetic heart of the system. We must never objectivise them, even in our unspoken thoughts.

It isn't enough that we don't 'operate' on them; we must always remember their courage in allowing us to learn from their willingness to expose their hopes and fears to us.

Convergent process

Convergent process is a recent development of the parallel process model. Figure 2.7 may appear complex at first, but it summarizes much we have learnt about what happens in supervision. It helps us track through the 'supervision space' any issues that may be driving the supervision problem.

The work-context for the client will show up in coaching, and any anomalies or 'wrinkles' can then be brought to supervision. By focusing what is going on, a key issue or theme will be identified. This may illuminate wider organisational concerns which can be dealt with. Typical examples are bullying or a lack of contracting, as illustrated by the stories below.

> In his coaching sessions, a recently-promoted client has difficulty in clarifying how he wants to work or what outcomes he wants. He spends a lot of time telling the story – without responding to interventions from his coach.
>
> When the coach talks to her supervisor, she too takes a lot of time giving the background – and is apparently unable to say what she wants from supervision.
>
> When her supervisor confronts her about this vagueness, she sees that her lack of precision is mirroring her client's.
>
> When, in turn, she talks with her client about their unclear contract, he realises his new work role is not sufficiently defined and that he is experiencing a lack of structure from his manager: he needs support to develop in his new job. He has been unwilling to admit to this anxiety, but as soon as he does he can see what he needs to do about it.

The actual experience of resistance to contracting in supervision has pinpointed the issue. Now the coach has recognised it, he can clarify the client's understanding of their own situation, and hopefully their work context as well.

> A supervisor starts to feel persecuted by their coach-supervisee. This shows up in a sense of discomfort as a new session approaches or a recurring sense of helpless resentment whilst working.
>
> When the supervisor shares this discomfort with the coach and they unravel their disrupted relationship together, this leads the coach to recognise that there is an unhealthy culture of harassment in the client's organisation. Having recognised this, the coach has options for how to respond.

So far, we have discussed the TA models of strokes, frame of reference, developmental stages, egostates, and games. We have also seen how they link to

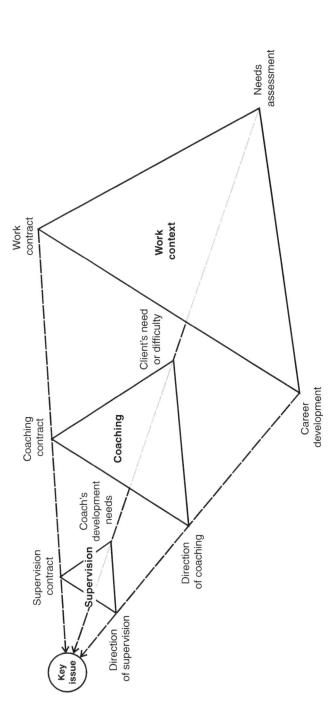

Figure 2.7   Convergent process.

parallel process, and so to the eight-eyed and convergent process models. In later chapters we will be introducing more TA ideas – relational needs and the supervision triangle, the place of life-script in the stories we all tell, the importance of contracting. But now we will look at the effects of applying TA ideas in various contexts.

Organisational culture

Since many coaches work internally or externally within organisations, it will be helpful to have a framework for picturing the organisational context of a coach's work. If they are working in several different organisations, these may differ in their cultural norms – and this will have a significant effect on the work the coach does with their clients.

PAC

One way of picturing an organisation is to return to the egostate model and use Parent, Adult and Child as metaphors for various aspects of the organisation[14]:

The Parent of the organisation is concerned with 'how we do things around here', and so –

- clarifies who we are;
- sets standards and guidelines for expected behaviour;
- maintains traditions and values for the organisation;
- implements systems of rewards and sanctions.

The Adult is concerned with procedures, and so –

- finds rational reasons for the organisation's behaviours and power structures;
- maintains the physical environment;
- uses inherited knowledge, skills and methods;
- implements planning, production and research.

The Child resources the character of the organisation, and so –

- gives emotional expression to the culture;
- maintains ways of relating personally and in groups through patterns of recognition and friendship;
- shows ways of experiencing and acting out acceptance or rejection, compliance or resistance;
- uses inherited ways of sabotaging or deviating from Parent expectations.

The organisational culture may be permissive or restrictive, work-oriented or not. We may unconsciously (and sometimes consciously) pick up clues from the way the organisation presents itself, both openly through work-place design, dress codes, public statements and so on, and more subtly through such things as social interactions and body language.

Our own frame of reference integrates our experiences, beliefs and expectations; it determines what we see and how we see it – and what we discount, or don't see. This is true for everyone, so we may find ourselves working with people and organisations whose frame is very different to our own.

Group imagos

The imago diagrams[15] in Figure 2.8 are an extremely useful way of mapping the coach's 'take' on an organisational culture and its impact on their client, and on them. Team coaches and supervisors working with groups of coaches can map the phases the group or team goes through as it develops.

Whenever we join a new group or team, we have some preconceptions about how it will be. We all have lots of experience of being part of a group; friends, family, colleagues or leisure activity – so we arrive with expectations based on our personal history or more recent encounters; these will be partly conscious, partly unconscious. We may 'project' these onto the group – or we take the opportunity to have a different experience this time!

So, we come along with a mental picture something like imago (a). We see ourselves, and probably the person in charge, but the rest remain a blur until we begin to meet and interrelate with them individually.

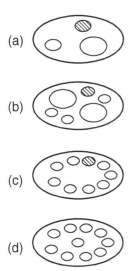

Figure 2.8 Imago diagrams.

Source: Napper and Newton 2014, 10:6–8.

As we do so, possibly rather formally at first, we update our picture to differentiate some group members according to our reactions to them ('Who does he remind me of?') and our increasing interactions with them ('Who can I connect with?', 'Is she interesting?', 'Does she like me?', Will I be left on my own?'). These questions are largely out of our awareness; they help us change our picture into one more like imago (b).

As a group develops over time, its members shift and eventually settle into more-or-less familiar roles: perhaps 'the helper', 'the one who has plenty to say – and always brings something for supervision', 'the quiet one', 'the one who doesn't say much but is perceptive when he does'. This is the stage where the psychological level can become apparent: is there competition for attention; are some people closer to the leader and/or supervisor? People by now know who everyone is imago (c), but there will be alliances and differences within the group.

We explore working with these imagos as a method of supervision in Chapter 7, where we see how the leader can enable a group to move through this sometimes painful stage to a situation where all its members work together well, support each other and focus on the purpose – with more equality in the group imago (d).

An ongoing group may well develop its own 'group's group imago'. Figure 2.9 is a picture of the shared norms and expectations in the group around rituals such as greetings, check-ins and endings, ways of working and relating to one another, the leader and/or supervisor, and beliefs about values, purposes or learning.

Do we expect to be 'filled' with information or look to the group leader to direct us, as in (a)? Do we think about the whole group and find we develop best

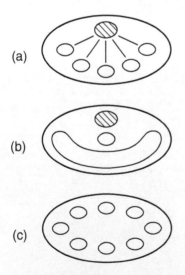

Figure 2.9   The group's group imago.

Source: Newton 2003.

when we do it with others as in (b)? Or, do we see all group members as equal contributors, including the leader, as in (c)?

In (a) the one-to-one relationship between leader and individual members of the group is primary; others are there, but not an influence. There is also a one-to-one relationship in (b) but others are now in support – and each has their turn to be at the focus. In (c) there is no one 'leader' – everyone is equally part of the process, no matter what their role.

If you supervise a group, think about which imago fits your group. In Chapter 7, we will introduce the 'tactile' imago, a way of modelling how a group is perceived and how this can be changed.

Making contact

You may be familiar with several ways of describing personality types. One model for understanding how we 'tune in to' others, which offers strategies for approaching people with different personalities, is known as 'Contact Doors' or 'Gateways'. This helps you to notice when communication is effective, understand why, and so decide how best to approach different individuals. It is a good way to get to know your supervisee.

Contact doors

Paul Ware has investigated how we contact each other.[16] He suggests that everyone has one particular way in which they prefer to be approached. To make successful contact we need to use the words, gestures, tone, facial expression, posture and gesture which are most welcome to each individual person.

He proposes that 'thinking', 'feeling' and 'doing' (behaviour) are three ways of being for which we each have our preferred order. These are like doors through which we can be successfully contacted – or that we may slam shut if wrongly approached. So, in a nutshell, we can best make contact with people through their thoughts, feelings or behaviour by noticing the kind of words they use when talking to us – and then responding similarly.

We all have our preferred order of thinking, feeling and doing, and these are the possible ones:

- thinking, feeling, doing;
- feeling, thinking, doing;
- doing, thinking, feeling;
- doing, feeling, thinking.

Note that 'doing' is never the middle, second option.

- The first door is where we have most energy available for a new relationship, our contact door.

- The next is the 'target' door, and this is the area where we can begin to make changes through supervision or coaching.
- The third of our doors, the 'trap' door, we protect from others and slam firmly shut if anyone taps on it too early in a relationship.

Listen carefully to simple conversations such as greetings.

When you say, 'How are you?' to someone, do they reply: 'I'm fine' or, 'I've done some good stuff today' or, 'I feel OK now' or, 'I'm better when the sun's shining' or, 'Yes, good, I think …'? You already have a clue to their contact door.

If they continue, 'I'm really keen to know what we're going to do in this session' or, 'How are you, you look like you're tired' or, 'I was thinking about what we talked about last time', you have yet more evidence.

Try out your hunch and start by using:

- 'Thinking' language: 'What ideas do you have?', 'Tell me your thoughts'.
- 'Feeling' language: 'What's your response to this?', 'Have you felt like this before?'.
- 'Doing' language: 'What happened?', 'What will you do next time?'.

If you are not sure, try using a mixture of words and see which they respond to most readily (Figure 2.10). It really does make a difference!

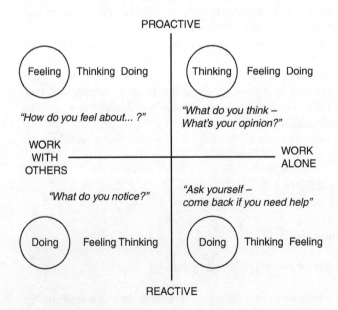

Figure 2.10   Assessing quadrant.

When you have established a connection by approaching someone through their contact door, they will be more confident in their relationship with you and ready to change how they see themselves and their situation.

> Think about how you like to be approached. Do you find any differences between your supervisees' preferences – or those of your colleagues?

Assessing, evaluating, judging

One of the challenges we have met in training supervisors for coaches is when the student is themselves a coach with – as an absolute foundation for their work – the belief that it is always wrong to 'judge' the client.

This may be expressed in terms of always offering unconditional positive regard, or some similar phrase. In transitioning to the role of supervisor, this will prove a hurdle to achieving a key function of the supervisor – 'assessment'.

The supervisor needs to be able to hold a place of continuous assessment, noticing where the supervisee is on their developmental journey, where they are strong and where they are more fragile. For a person to really grow as a supervisor, they need to develop an ability to assess their own work in a way that is critical (i.e. informed and intelligent) though non-judgemental.

This is an important part of coaching being respected as a profession: its practitioners are open to the challenge to develop. Attending supervision is probably the key activity for coaches in terms of their CPD (Continuing Professional Development), particularly as there are still very few extended or advanced coach trainings available in this area.

Increasingly, coach supervisors are being asked to provide a reference (typically annually) for a coach – to their professional body, to an associate group or a directly employing organisation. These references may vary in terms of the depth of observation required, from 'How often do they have supervision and in what way?' to, 'Do they have a good understanding of the organisational context in which they work?'

As a supervisor, you will obviously make your own decision about where the boundaries are, and we suggest this is done in conversation with your supervisee.

- What are your own feelings about assessment?
- What is the place of this competence for you within your role as supervisor?
- Do you feel that you yourself (or your coach supervisees) have benefited from assessment by another adult who is 'wiser and stronger in the moment' – and how does this phrase land with you?

Choosing your own approach

All the above has provided you with some background on the perspectives, frameworks and philosophies that give each of us our unique identities as supervisors

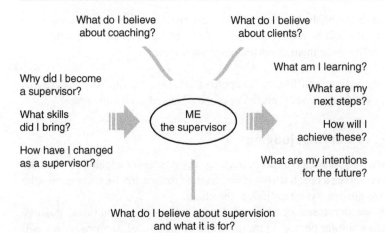

Figure 2.11   Self-awareness framework.

Source: Adapted from Temple 1999.

and/or coaches. You may have your own preferred way of working, or you may choose to vary your approach depending on the experience of your supervisee and the context in which you are both working.

In this chapter, we have discussed the frameworks and theories we can use when thinking about supervision, and in Chapter 7, we will look at how these can be used in our actual work.

Before reading on, you might like to use Figure 2.11 to reflect on your developing identity as a supervisor.

We have provided a number of suggestions and models which you can use to underpin your practice as a supervisor – and we expect you already have a rich and varied toolbox that you bring to this role, so:

- What are you already trained in?
- What are your own models, and how can you integrate them into your practice as a supervisor?
- When you look at your career and your experience to date, what do you notice that will serve you and your clients well? And, how will this inform the development of your unique identity as a coach supervisor?

Saša's story

Saša showed up for supervision somewhat anxious. She wanted to talk about a client she was disappointed in – who wasn't using this great coaching opportunity to do serious work. The client was a senior leader in an organisation where a coaching programme was being run by a colleague of Saša's – who had asked her to work with three of the group.

So, going into the work, the stakes were high – Saša always wants to do a really good job, but this felt even more important because she couldn't let her colleague down or in any way damage her reputation.

Two of Saša's clients were coming along nicely. They were enthusiastic and engaged in the process, working hard in between sessions, willing to go to real depths within themselves in order to understand their behaviour and challenge themselves to significant personal growth.

The third client, the subject of this supervision, was different: he came to his sessions enthusiastically and wanted Saša to give him tools, tasks to take away. When he reported back, he had always used the tools and completed the tasks … and things were going really well for him. That was until the very end of the most recent session, when he briefly mentioned that he might have the odd problem.

Saša felt he wasn't taking the coaching sufficiently seriously and that he wasn't challenging himself at a personal level. She was worried that he was going to report back that the coaching wasn't of much value.

She wasn't looking forward to the rest of their sessions, so in supervision she wanted to get to the bottom of what was going on for her; what was stopping her giving of her best with this client.

When we explored more, it transpired that Saša had been doing a lot of work supervising and mentoring coaches who had opted to work with her and were invested in their own development, both professionally and personally. She said, 'They really want to learn and grow – and to look long and hard at themselves – doesn't everyone?'

Well, everyone apart from this client!

We talked about two things: one was her frame of reference, starting with 'Everyone …' – Well, perhaps not 'everyone', and perhaps not someone who's been sent for coaching in a corporate environment.

Secondly, we looked at contact doors: Saša's client was showing up, asking questions, doing the work, telling her he really valued the tools she was offering him. He was indicating that he was willing to show some vulnerability, to reveal things that were more difficult for him and ask for support on them. In fact, the person who was dissatisfied was Saša.

So, in her supervision session, Saša allowed herself to step away and look at the work that was actually happening with this client. She had been building rapport and trust; she had been adding value in a very real way, and had created the opportunity for him to challenge himself in further sessions to grow even more.

What had been getting in the way was Saša's own anxiety about her performance. She had limited her frame of reference to just one part of her client group, and was frustrated that this client's way of making contact was through fact-based input and a light, positive outlook.

Saša has begun to realise that she has the capability to meet this client where he is, to offer him what he needs now, and to build a relationship which will support his future growth.

And, she knows that she can do it in a light way. She just needed reminding of the breadth of her own experience, and the fact that it's OK to be a lot of fun.

Notes

1   Thanks to Pete Shotton for this quote.
2   Thanks to Patrick Hobbs for this extract from notes on his supervision philosophy.
3   The idea of 'frame of reference' comes from the work of Jacqui Schiff and the Cathexis school of TA. The frame of reference includes the script or life-script, discussed in Chapter 4, Learning in relationship. Jean Illsley Clarke developed the idea to include levels of influence, from deep (unconscious) often cultural levels of impact to more those available to scrutiny and therefore more easily changeable.
4   There are a number of books available that give a good overview of TA concepts. *Into TA* (Cornell *et al.* 2016) is a new and comprehensive textbook covering all fields of application and all levels of understanding from basic to latest theory and including articles on practical case-studies by active practitioners in all fields. A relational perspective and a chapter-by-chapter coaching case-study can be found in Lapworth and Sills (2011) and a work-based approach in *Working it out at Work* by Julie Hay. *Tactics* explores TA concepts for adult educators with many practical examples and exercises. Details of these and other TA books can be found in Further Reading and in the bibliography.
5   For more on strokes and endorphins, see Gerhardt *Why Love Matters*.
6   There are several psychological models of stages of human development from childhood to old age – perhaps Erikson's is the best known. The one we use here is from the work of Pamela Levin (Levin-Landheer 1982). The value of Levin's model lies in its cyclic nature – the premise that we re-cycle the stages throughout life and can therefore 're-do' any that were difficult or incomplete for us in childhood or adolescence. For each developmental stage there are 'tasks' to be accomplished and supportive affirmations that enable us to complete them. The original model has been developed for many applications – parenting, for schools, in adult education and in management of change for organisations, among others.
7   Models of egostates (of which there are many) differentiate between the structural (what is there) and the functional (how we act on it). Mary Cox's diagram (1999) makes clear the link between the two – the positive behaviours derived from all egostates and the choices we can make in Adult to employ them appropriately. We have drawn on Cox's work in creating the diagram shown in Figure 2.3.
8   Keith Tudor writes about the Integrating Adult in Sills and Hargaden 2003 and in *Co-creative Transactional Analysis* (Tudor & Summers 2014).
9   Berndt Schmid won the Eric Berne Memorial Award in 2003 for his work on roles in relation to egostates.
10   In 2004 Agnes Le Guernic proposed that there is a 'normal' triangle underlying the drama triangle, representing children's social learning.
11   The 'Drama Triangle' was first published in an article by Steve Karpman in 1968, based on an analysis of stories, from fairy stories and folk tales to Greek drama, modern novels and films. All have their Persecutors, Rescuers and Victims, and the switches between them drive the plot (think of any *James Bond* film). Later, Acey Choy proposed a positive version, the *winners' triangle*, which builds on the OK component of each role. To stay on the winners' triangle we need both recognition for the reality of our experience and support in making changes.
12   'Parallel process' is the term generally used for what Searles in 1955 called a 'reflection process'. Recently, Beinart and Clohessy (2017 p. 39) have suggested a similar process, 'isomorphism', which they describe as a relational concept used in *systemic* understanding, as opposed to the psycho-dynamic, intra-psychic construct understanding of parallel process.

13 In the first edition of their classic book, *Supervision in the Helping Professions*, Hawkins and Shohet proposed the 'double matrix' model to show the various areas of attention in the supervision process. They later developed this into the now famous '7-eyed model', which extended it to include the context or environment as a factor to be accounted. The version we use is based on one drawn by Alistair Nee; by turning the diagram to make it horizontal equality and mutuality in working practice are emphasised.

14 The metaphor of PAC in organisational culture began with Berne in *Structure and Dynamics of Organisations and Groups* (1963), his one book on transactional analysis in organisations, and was later elaborated by Pearl Drego and applied to social as well as organisational culture (1983).

15 Imago theory was first described by Berne in *Structure and Dynamics*, see note 14. Berne writes about the way groups maintain themselves in their context – the power of external pressure and the internal cohesion that resists the pressure, the internal agitation that can disrupt the group, and the balance that each member strives for between their own desires and the wish to be part of the group. The imago model is part of this, showing the mental picture that each member holds and how it develops. Healthy groups will move through the stages, less healthy groups may get stuck in the third stage and continue competition and agitation (or occasionally even be stuck in the second stage and never move beyond tentative contact – such groups will not last long if the task is supervision). Clarke built on these imagos by proposing that whole groups develop joint imagos that represent the group culture (1996). Newton (2003) describes such 'group's group imagos' for learning groups.

16 The idea of 'doors to contact' originated with Paul Ware and later became incorporated in the personality adaptations model. This is explored in detail by Joines and Stewart in their book *Personality Adaptations* (2002), based on the work of Ware and Taibi Kahler.

Chapter 3

Relational needs

The supervision triangle

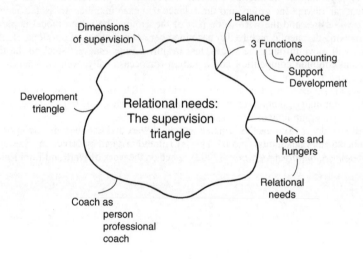

... to make meaning in the work in the service of self, client and system.[1]

'Self, client and system', 'ourselves, others and the world'. So often we find that triple note in what we say and how we see things. Photographers and artists use three points when composing a photo or drawing, to create interest, for balance and, sometimes, to show tension between elements. We 'get' the picture because, somehow, the three points of a triangle make for a satisfying image.

This book contains many instances of the number three: Parent-Adult-Child, the drama, winners and social roles triangles, doing-thinking-feeling and, in Chapter 5, we will explore the three-cornered contract.

In the previous chapter, we asked, 'What is supervision?', comparing it with mentoring and coaching. We distinguished between practice analysis and supervision or, to put it another way, 'task and relationship'. Here we move on to look at the question, 'What is supervision for?' and introduce the supervision triangle, a model that offers:

- A map of supervision, both for planning and for reflecting.
- An integrating framework – the triangle can be used to integrate a number of themes within supervision and can be a meta-model for the overview and analysis of practice.
- Guidance for new or beginning supervisors – new supervisors often struggle to find a way to monitor their own practice, their identity and philosophy. This triangle promotes the critique and conscious improvement of less developed areas.
- A check that we are doing ethical supervision – supervision which only concentrates on one or two aspects is unfair to the supervisee. Using the triangle as a tool encourages self and mutual reflection in the supervisory relationship.

But before we introduce the triangle, we will describe why we need it.

The supervision request

A colleague says that sometimes, when working with a supervisee with whom she has created trust and 'a reliable level of intimacy' – she asks herself, 'How come I am the one who gets paid?'

Her answer is that it is because she is in the role of supervisor: she is responsible for keeping the meta-perspective, for overseeing the process rather than entering into it at the risk of losing that perspective.

Sometimes the supervisee brings such interesting and challenging supervision problems that she feels tempted to get into the debate; sometimes this impulse is so strong that, as she says, 'My only hope of retaining the meta-level perspective is to admit to the impulse and bring that part of myself into the public arena'.[2] This is what makes the discussion real: to admit that we have all the responses we are experiencing, and to demand that the supervisee be equally honest; to agree that we both will disclose anything that might be relevant to understanding what is getting in the way of the supervisee forging ahead with their own ideas, preferences, impulses – in accordance with their own values.

This 'making the discussion real' seems to be related to the supervisor 'not knowing' and yet still being able to hold open the door and show the way to a meta-perspective.

This is an important idea: there is a job to be done – both supervisor and supervisee will have relational needs within the supervision context. The supervisor must constantly self-monitor to enable both the task and the relationship to be furthered.

The job of the supervisor is to hold a stable frame as a guide to their choice of intervention, and to help the supervisee identify (or create) their own frame. These frames will vary from the 'training' supervision of inexperienced practitioners to the 'reliable intimacy' of colleagues with similar levels of experience. In either case, the supervisee does the needed work within the supervisory discussion and the supervisor is present as a supportive witness to this deeply intra-personal happening. This process, and witnessing to it, is often a key to answering the supervision request.

The supervisee will have needs and expectations of supervision – to be safe, supported, validated, encouraged and so on – and the supervisor will have needs as well. These may not always be recognised, but they will nevertheless impact the process. Supervisor and supervisee may have very different (unconscious) answers to the question 'What is supervision for?'

From the supervisor's perspective, this means recognising the need for ongoing awareness of the patterns and dynamics of the supervision.

> Like in a dance, they regulate closeness and distance, autonomy and the need for impact from the other, the need to feel accepted, and maybe the need to appreciate others and to express it.
>
> In that dance, sometimes the supervisor will facilitate the learning of coaching practice and there she will usually meet present-oriented relational needs. Sometimes, she supports the personal development of the supervisee or tries to offer a healing experience, where she will perhaps encounter different needs, for reassurance or acceptance. Sometimes, she will challenge the supervisee to explore the meaning of the ways the needs have become apparent. And, all the time she will be experiencing her own needs, for impact on the supervisee, for contact, for satisfaction.
>
> The supervisor who accepts and works with these not only provides a healthy model for her supervisees, but is usually a more integrated and congruent practitioner.[3]

The functions of supervision – needs and hungers

All human beings have basic physiological needs for food and water, physical safety, warmth and rest. But we also have psychological needs, part of the universal human desire for relationship and attachment.

Berne noted the hungers[4] that we all experience: our existential need for stimulus, for recognition, and our hunger for structure are the starting point of the theories he developed about strokes, transactions, games and script. These needs underlie all our actions in the world and are part of who we are – no matter what strategies we devise, successful or otherwise, to get them met. We can develop this idea of 'relational' needs to include acceptance, validation, affirmation, significance, having an impact on others.

If these 'hungers' are so essential to us, taking account of them is a part of good supervision and self-supervision. We need an overall balance between stimulation, recognition and certainty (or safety) in our work and in the flow of a session.

Security, acceptance and impact are crucial to our thinking about supervision, and we can relate them to the functions of supervision and the triangle model. To explore these three functions further, we can look at the different ways in which they have been described in various contexts.

The idea that supervision has three main functions was first suggested by Kadushin (1976), and this has been taken up with variations by several other writers.

In the context of social work, Kadushin highlighted the importance of managerial supervision and the need for support and learning opportunities for staff. After showing how earlier ideas about supervision focused on the mentoring of newer staff and maintaining the standards of the agency, he concluded that its true functions are administration, support and education.

- The aim of administration is to ensure the implementation of agency policies and procedures.
- The aim of support is to promote the improvement of morale and job satisfaction (presumably the problem being that these are often rather low).
- And, for education, the problem is the ignorance or ineptitude of workers; the goal being to dispel these.

This rather depressing view of supervision was lightened, along with a change of terminology, when Brigid Proctor (2000) applied the ideas to counselling supervision as an 'alliance' model – a task framework with responsibility shared between supervisor and supervisee for normative (monitoring standards and ethics), restorative (refreshment) and formative (facilitating learning) tasks. In discussing group supervision, she suggests that awareness of these tasks emphasises the shared responsibility of all participants – as well as the supervisor.

Hawkins and Smith (2006) recognised the different contexts of these sets of terms. They suggest that, for coaching, the functions are better described as 'qualitative, resourcing and developmental'.

In essence, these three main functions of supervision address the needs of all practitioners, coaches, counsellors, therapists and educators. We have chosen some new terms: 'accounting' (for all parties, a meta-perspective, which includes organisational supervision), 'nurturative' (offering recognition and encouragement as well as support) and 'transformative' (describing the thrill and excitement of supervision when new pathways open up).

All these terms are shown together in Table 3.1. In the rest of this chapter, we use 'management', 'support' and 'development', alongside accounting, nurture and transformation, according to the context.

Table 3.1 The functions of supervision

NEED/HUNGER	KADUSHIN (1976)	PROCTOR (2000)	HAWKINS (2006)	NEWTON (2012)
STRUCTURE security	Managerial	Normative	Qualitative	Accounting
RECOGNITION acceptance	Supportive	Restorative	Resourcing	Nurturative
STIMULUS impact	Educative	Formative	Developmental	Transformative

Adapted from Newton 2012, p. 104.

Whatever we choose to call them, these three functions acknowledge our need for structure, recognition and stimulus, and that this is why supervisors and writers on supervision continue to use the same idea in various forms.

We all want contact with other people and are motivated to be in meaningful and satisfying relationships; we need the information-feedback of stimulus in order to grow, the organising of our experience through structure so that we can create meaning, and the reinforcement of our belief in self and others through recognition. If any one of these is lacking, we may compensate by overdoing one of the others – for example, over-structuring to make up for a perceived deficit of recognition.

Let's explore the three parts of supervision in more detail.

Accounting

The accounting (or 'accounting for') function provides an oversight on the work, making sure it is appropriate to the context and the contract, is ethical and is conducted to a suitable standard.

Depending on the context, this may include taking account of the organisational multi-cornered contract, the level of the practitioner's competence and potential boundary issues. The focus is kept on the purpose of the work, if and how the multi-cornered contract has become skewed, and it brings to light any blind spots, assumptions or prejudices that the supervisee may have been unaware of. This is very relevant when looking at the various expectations of coaches coming to supervision: sometimes there is a desire to be 'told', or the experience of adapting to a hierarchical culture.

Nurture

The nurturative function provides emotional support for the coach to deal with the intensity of working with clients and the inevitable pressures of being attentive and empathic. Coaches also need to attend to themselves – supervision offers a safe space within which they can recognise their own needs and the risks of collusion, burn-out and somatic reaction to stress. This function takes account of the stage of development of the coach and may be a key part of supervision for beginners – but it is still essential for experienced workers.

Transformation

The transformative function promotes reflection and exploration around how to implement theory, hone practice and take up the challenge to become ever more aware of one's own and others' reactions and responses – and so to increase understanding and options for intervention.

This may include growing through further training, choosing new inputs or methods and developing an individual identity and autonomy. Here, the supervisee can create their own unique ways of working, choose their next steps in development, and self-supervise (with a supervisor and/or a group as participating witnesses).

Introducing the supervision triangle

Whenever we create and deliver training programmes for coach-supervisors, one model, the supervision triangle (Figure 3.1)[5] – a visual representation of the three functions of supervision – is a key feature of the training. We believe this model is also valuable to supervisors of counsellors, therapists, consultants and educators, so we will describe it here as being of general application.

The supervision triangle is a model of the necessary balance of the three functions and a caution of the risk of over-emphasising one at the expense of the others: too much rigidity, cosiness or scare may result. These risks of 'too much' are, of course, matched by the risks of 'too little' – which may give rise to a sense of abandonment, isolation, or lack of connection.

Why draw a triangle? Well, it's a bit like a three-legged stool – if any one leg collapses, the stool is completely useless. The three corners need to be balanced to be effective. Sometimes, there will be an emphasis on one corner, because that is what is needed at that moment – for instance, Support for a coach encountering serious trauma in a client, or Management of an obvious boundary issue – but if

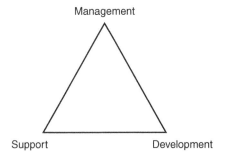

Figure 3.1   The supervision triangle.

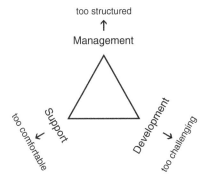

Figure 3.2   The balance of supervision functions.

Source: Newton and Napper 2007, p. 151.

one corner dominates over time then the 'stool' begins to topple and, what's more, the dominating corner will have an effect that both supervisee and supervisor may notice, as in Figure 3.2.

Turning the three functions into the corners of a triangle, makes it more accessible (and not only for visual learners), shows up connections and encourages new ideas. As an equilateral triangle, the balance or equilibrium between the functions is demonstrated. Altogether, the triangle becomes much more than a simple list of aspects of supervision and offers a more satisfying framework for understanding what goes on in supervision: a meta-perspective providing a reference point or internal check for experienced supervisors as well as guidance for beginning supervisors.

Why does this triangle have such an impact? Partly because the three functions are related to three characteristic parts of the human personality: our sense of responsibility to others and ourselves, our need for contact and recognition as individual selves, our ability to grow and change as we meet and assess new situations. A second reason for the 'rightness' of the triangle is that it takes account of our existential human need for stimulus, our desire for recognition, and our hunger for structure and certainty.

The 'resonance' or rightness of this model helps to integrate several aspects of supervision theory and, almost every time we present it, groups come up with new developments: a real example of praxis, reflective practice and theory working together (we will explore some of these developments when we consider the three corners in more detail).

One group of beginning supervisors proposed additions to the three points of the triangle linked to different aspects of the coach's development, as shown in Figure 3.3.

Depending on the sort of person we are, all of us have a tendency towards one of the corners: do we want to help and nurture others; are we concerned about accountability and ethics; do we find newness and growth exciting? We may even choose how we do supervision (and coaches may choose the supervisors they like to work with) because of a particular emphasis. Our own ways of seeing supervision and the frameworks we prefer may follow from these preferences.

Coach as professional

Coach as person   Coach as coach

Figure 3.3   Roles on the supervision triangle.

Getting to an understanding of our own preferences can help us to be alert to the risks of paying too much attention to 'our' corner and neglecting the other two.

Coach as person: support and nurture

Our way of seeing supervision will vary according to how we think about it and what aspects of it we prioritise – our ways of working and the frameworks we choose as reference points will follow.

First, let's think about new coaches or coaches in training:

There's a lot of influence here from the humanistic tradition, with its emphasis on support of the supervisee and nurturing of their personal growth. There is a strong awareness of the stages of development that practitioners go through in becoming effective, and supervision is tailored to appropriate interventions for each stage. The focus is on the person, while community and organisational perspectives are less in evidence. The role of the supervisor is nurturative – who (and where on their journey) is this person as a practitioner, and what do they need?

Several models for supervision denote stages that coaches in training go through.[6]

First, there is the stage of acquiring skills and learning how to use them; the focus will be on the coach themselves as a new practitioner; their work may feel clunky, and they may well be practising on friends and co-learners.

As they become more fluent, their focus will move to the client: What does the client need? How can the coach meet this need? At this stage, the coach may be working with 'real' clients and observing their own development in supervision.

Later, the focus becomes the relationship: what happens between us? How is this pertinent to the client's outcomes? This can sometimes become a trap, as in the following example:

> I knew that I needed some supervision on my work with one particular coach. Every session, we seemed to go over the same ground – talking about different clients, but with such similar problems in her work with them. I felt stuck as a supervisor, and I didn't seem to be able to do anything different. So, each time I supervised this coach I felt as though I was getting through the time rather than enabling any growth or change. As I described this tedious process, my supervisor asked, 'How do you feel?'
>
> How did I feel? I felt bored! I didn't want to work with a coach who didn't grow. But maybe I was letting that happen – by falling into the trap of reassuring her that she was doing fine, even though I didn't think she was.

My supervisee and I were stuck in the support corner: the coach needed reassurance and I was giving it – not as a base for moving on, but as the only point of supervision. The support corner had become the place we went to in each session; she felt comfortable there and not challenged – I felt uninvolved.

In reality, we needed to do some work on her competence and over-availability to clients, so that she could put in boundaries and contract more appropriately – and, of course, exactly the same applied to her supervisor.

A valuable model for the support of new coaches is the stages of development and cycles model, described in Chapter 2: when we take on something new, we seem to go through the stages of development afresh – a mini-cycle – as if we are being 're-born' into the new situation.[7]

As you read this next bit, think about a recent time when something changed for you; a new piece of work, a new job, moving to a new area:

- At first, we have a sense almost of shock: competence (and maybe energy) drop for a while – 'what have I taken on?'
- Then, as we go on, we start to draw on our previous learning and experience and have some success – so our energy rises and we gain in confidence.
- But sooner or later (usually sooner), we hit a situation that we can't deal with, or that goes wrong. So we get frustrated: we need to do something differently, but we don't know how. This is the 'frustration dip'.
- At this point, supervision is key: the supervisor can help us to think through our stuckness (without doing the thinking for us) and enable us to discover our own way of coaching, create our individual identity as a coach and concentrate on learning how to do the work better.

Even though they may feel uncomfortable, we need to go through these stages: once that dip has been navigated and the coach begins to create their own unique identity, further development and integration of new ideas means that competence rises, reaching the optimum of an autonomous and potent coach – being the best coach they can.

At the same time as they are supporting a coach through this learning process, the supervisor may be going through it themselves as a new supervisor; for instance, they may be needing support in thinking through how to do some aspect of supervision differently.

This is not to suggest that we only need support in supervision when we are new to coaching. Everyone can encounter difficulties, feel 'not up to it', stuck, overburdened or simply want to 'off-load' in a sympathetic environment and be supported in developing further.

Thinking through the stages can be a useful tool here too: it helps identify the nature of the problem and what the supervisee needs in order to resolve it; is the coach overwhelmed, denying a need for more information, unable to think clearly through something, developing a new aspect of their work? Do they need to feel welcome, to have time to explore, to have someone to think alongside them or challenge their decisions, to encourage new development or to witness to their individuality?

However, the 'support' corner is a place where Rescuing or Parenting can easily happen, particularly when the coach comes with a Child need or scare. The boundary between authentic support and rescuing can be quite finely drawn and needs to be carefully negotiated.

Coach as professional: accounting and management

Many supervisors prioritise observable change in their supervisees. The approach here can be derived from behavioural psychology – quite structured, with an emphasis on competence, criteria and standards; with a stress on attention to the protection of the client, on ethical perspectives and professional suitability.

Models of supervision that highlight this function tend to be 'grounded' and workman-like. Coaches will be familiar with models such as 'CLEAR'[8] and 'GROW',[9] and may be expecting a similar formula to be used in their own supervision – and certainly this kind of framework can provide a basic structure.

The 'management' approach is essential in developing high levels of competence and skills fitting for the profession. The role of the supervisor may include assessment – what does this supervisee need to do in order to coach effectively? Is the work they are doing appropriate to the situation?

Useful tools for this approach include lists of competencies and criteria such as the ICF Coaching Competencies and checklists for supervision such as the one described in Chapter 5:

- Has the key issue been identified?
- Has the contract been fulfilled?
- What about the context and the contract the coach is working in, and the appropriateness and level of the work?

One version of the supervision checklist includes 'emotional contact' – which is as important in Management as in the other corners of the supervision triangle.

In the various roles that a supervisor may take up, depending on the context and the present-moment need of the supervisee, informing, guiding, coaching and challenging can be part of the 'menu' contracted-for at the time, even if this approach is not a usual part of the supervisory relationship.

We may tend to think about the supervision triangle in terms of what is needed in the session and where our supervisee is most (and least) comfortable. However, as supervisors, we have to ask ourselves how we feel about each corner: we'll almost certainly have an instinctive bias, and indeed there are some styles of supervision which can only operate out of one corner.

Taking care to understand our own comfort and discomfort helps us not to collude with our supervisee. It may also help us to understand whether we want to be a supervisor at all!

One coach on a supervision training course came to the conclusion that, for her, having to operate out of the management corner and needing at times to tell the supervisee, 'You must stop doing this', or to stand behind their work and give a written reference, was just so far outside her own beliefs and working practices as a coach that she couldn't – and wouldn't – continue to do it. She therefore decided that working as a supervisor was not for her.

Even more intriguing is what can happen to the supervisor when the client challenges them in one of the corners.

I noticed this for myself when I had a supervisee who always started our sessions with lots of questions about me – what had I been doing, how was I feeling, how was work going for me?

At the surface level, I asked her to stop doing this. It was taking precious time from her supervision session, which she was paying for herself, and which I knew was important to her.

We also talked about whether this indicated her need to rescue – which we both knew was instinctive for her.

It took me much longer to acknowledge that I myself was incredibly uncomfortable about someone genuinely caring about me, as a person, in the context of a professional relationship.

Changing the way we connected each time was now working for me but for her, I was refusing to acknowledge her preferred contact door (feeling) and her genuine desire to express her care for a person she liked and respected.

Coach as coach: development and transformation

As a supervisor, you might want to focus on the coach as a professional and use the perspective above, or the coach as a person and take a humanistic approach. But a third perspective to consider is 'the coach as coach': how does supervision promote the coach in growing, developing and becoming the best they can be?

This approach draws on radical educational philosophy: it is closely related to constructivist and co-creative approaches to the learning process. Its emphasis is on the developmental function of supervision, especially as a transformative experience – mutually so for both the supervisee and supervisor. Reflective, theory-to-practice working ('praxis') is the basis for creating new narratives about the supervision process.

A key model here is the learning cycle and its connection with life-script and narrative. This model is so significant in our thinking and our training that we have devoted the next chapter to it (Chapter 4), so at this point we will mention just one aspect of the model: 'action research'.

What does action research mean for supervision?

As we go through the supervision process, supervisor and supervisee (or a group of supervisees) are in effect employing a method of reflective practice akin to the learning cycle: each piece of supervision is an experience to be reflected on, 'data' to be scrutinised.

This reflection leads to formulating an idea about how to proceed – maybe by doing something differently next time. Then the effect of this can be evaluated, and further changes made if necessary.

This is the essence of research: each piece of work builds up the store of data about what works and what needs changing. The knowledge so gained may be fed back into the system to benefit clients, organisations, even the whole coaching profession.

Supervisees are also 'learning about learning' by being aware of the value of this experiential system for creating understanding. Everyone becomes partners in a collaboration which, in itself, helps to create new methods and insights for supervision. These ideas are brought together in Figure 3.4.

You will see that we have added 'P, A, C' to the corners: the metaphorical Parent takes account of the socially responsible aspects of supervision; the Child need for personal recognition is met by the nurturing/support function; the Adult is expanded through the challenge of transformative learning.

Coach as professional

ACCOUNTING
MANAGEMENT

Contracts – ethics – organisations & contexts – boundaries and responsibilities – imagos – meeting standards / competencies / criteria

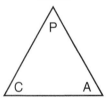

Coach as person	Coach as coach
NURTURE SUPPORT	TRANSFORMATION DEVELOPMENT
Supervisory relationship – process and dynamics – script – parallel process – reflection, review – supervision of supervision – developmental stages	Action research – learning cycle/reflective practice – exploring methods, models and philosophies – personal experience and 'tools' – developing competencies – self-assessment – narrative – co-creation

Figure 3.4   Dimensions of supervision.

Source: Based on Cochrane and Newton 2011, p. 14.

Developing potency

As well as offering protection and giving appropriate permission, we believe that part of the job of a supervisor is to enable the supervisee to experience their own potency, so we can say that protection is linked to management, permission to support – and potency to development.[10]

The supervisee's growth and development are built on sound support and management: just as any individual's potency is grounded in safety and affirmation, so a supervisee's developing professional identity and autonomy need a base of ethical accounting and collegial support.

The process of supervision enables the supervisee to build their own internal protection, permission and potency through attention to each corner. If we turn the triangle around and combine it with the three 'p's, we can see the importance of accounting and support in promoting development (Figure 3.5).

The supervisee's experience of their own potency and autonomy will grow from a sense of being safe enough, and having enough permission, to be themselves, to create their own way of working, to explore and to experiment (Figure 3.6).[11]

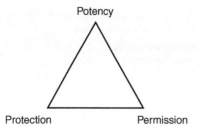

Figure 3.5   The autonomy triangle.

Source: Deconinck 1994, personal communication.

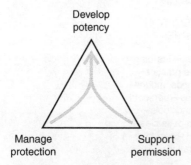

Figure 3.6   The developmental supervision triangle.

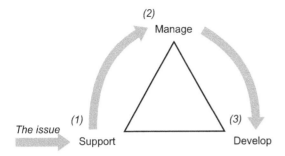

Figure 3.7   An example of flow in supervision.

Flow and the triangle

Whichever way we prefer to draw the supervision triangle, it is not static. There are various entry points. Someone may come with a problem that seems to require support but, as the dialogue goes on, a tricky ethical issue appears and so we shift to accounting. Or, the story seems to be about difficulties in a team – until it uncovers the supervisee's own deep anxiety about not being up to the task.[12]

It's rather like the 'dance' we mentioned at the beginning of this chapter – a continuing flow between the three corners, moving together, then apart; taking in different perspectives until a harmony is created. In the diagram in Figure 3.7 we show an example – the 'entry' issue appears as a need for support ('I'm not up to this task'), but in the exploration the discussion moves to management (the contract is not clear or not being held to by someone) and then, as the underlying dilemma is revealed, on to development (I can find my own way to do this!).

Bringing it all together

As you will have realised by now, this triangle is central to our view of all types of supervision, and especially to teaching the skills and ethos of supervision. Not only is it a key model and reference framework to assist the supervisor in their work, it enables us to connect with many other topics related to supervision. Everything we want to share can be related to the supervision triangle and to the importance of taking account of all three corners.

So, what are we doing when we do supervision? This triangle enables us to give a focus to our question and clarify the sometimes sprawling range of material that comes under the heading of 'supervision'. It's not a replacement for other methods and models, but it underpins them; and, in doing so, it is no threat to 'old favourite' or freshly-created models: it offers a way of checking on their validity and value.

The 'congruence' of the supervision triangle is a source of the sense of satisfaction that supervisees experience – it addresses relational needs, individual preferences, the three 'p's of protection, permission and potency; it has the capacity to encompass a variety of perspectives – doing, thinking and feeling – and it connects to a range of perceptions of supervision.

Notes

1 Thanks to Jenny Bird.
2 Thanks to Mary Cox for her reflections on being a supervisor, published in TAJ in 2007.
3 Nevenka Miljkovic modified the ideas of Richard Erskine on relational needs to fit them to adult learning. We have drawn on her work in this chapter.
4 In his first real transactional analysis book, *Transactional Analysis in Psychotherapy*, Eric Berne noted the hungers that all human beings experience (1961, p. 83). The existential need for stimulus, followed by the need for recognition, and the hunger for structure are the base of the theories he developed about strokes, transactions, games and script.
5 The supervision triangle as such appears for the first time in TAJ 37:2, as a model of the necessary *balance* of the three functions and a caution of the risk of over-emphasising one at the expense of the others (Newton & Napper 2007). A complete TAJ article devoted to it was published in 2012 (Newton 2012).
6 Examples (from counselling/therapy supervision) are Stoltenberg and Delworth 1987 *Supervising Counselors and Therapists: A developmental approach* San Francisco: Josey-Bass Wiley, and Richard Erskine 1982 Supervision of Psychotherapy: Models for Professional Development TAJ 12:4.
7 Pam Levin's work on developmental stages was developed into a model for understanding change by Julie Hay (Hay 1993).
8 See Hawkins and Smith (2006).
9 A simple method for goal setting and problem solving – Goals, Reality, Obstacles, Options, Way forward.
10 Claude Steiner wrote about the three 'p's – protection, permission and potency – in *Scripts People Live* (1974) Chapter 21. The first two are positive Parent functions that enable the (therapy) client to develop their own potency. The idea also applies in supervision.
11 Jacques Dekoninck described the education or autonomy triangle in a workshop in 1994.
12 Thanks to the many colleagues and students who have added their ideas in the development of the supervision triangle and its uses, and especially to Patrick Hobbs for the idea of 'flow'.

Chapter 4

Learning in relationship

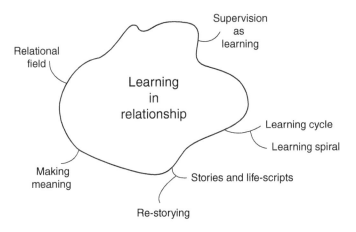

If someone tells you a story, they are no longer a stranger.[1]

Learning is how we change; we learn from one another in dialogue, in relationship:

A few years ago, I took part in a piece of research asking new supervisors about what had been important to them as they moved towards accreditation, and their experience of their emergent role. Most important to them was the relationship with their own supervisors, both as individuals and among their peers in supervision groups. This was where they identified their most significant and heartfelt learning about themselves, their practice and how these connect. This research gave them an opportunity to reflect with others on how and why this was the case.

Supervision, both in training and ongoing practice, is an archetypical example of experiential learning: we learn by reflecting on lived experience. This is how growth and healing can happen for practitioner, client and supervisor too. This is the essence of properly functioning supervision.

To put up some scaffolding to support our thinking, we will explore the links between supervision and:

- how we make meaning;
- learning as a relational, co-creative means for change;
- stories, life-script and the learning cycle.

The vitality of storytelling

Stories are important, to us and to everyone. Human beings are all story-tellers; it's how we begin to create our own picture of the world when we are small – by listening to stories, making up our own and telling them to those around us.

Stories are how we learn to make meaning, to understand other people, to bring our feelings and thoughts to life. This is what literature is about: making conscious and 'relatable' all our cares, highs and lows, exhilarations – everything that makes us who we are as individuals and as part of a human community.

You will have noticed there are many stories in this book: we use them to illustrate, to ask questions, to connect practice, experience, reflection and theory.

When I read short stories by for instance Alice Munro or novels by Anita Brookner, I am struck by how, whatever their particular characters and wherever in the world the stories are set, they seem to be part of the same narrative – of loss, of leaving, and sometimes of love.

We hear many stories in supervision. Time and again it will seem to be the same story – even though the characters and the settings change (though, of course, the supervisee is always the protagonist). The overarching narrative, as it shows up in these 'little picture' stories, tells us the theme – or, if you prefer, the script.

So let's think for a moment about narratives and stories within them.

Our supervision 'narratives' reflect both where we have come from and why we do things the way we do – our values, and our beliefs that everyone matters; that being available and vulnerable, working in a relationship of compassion and mutuality, is key; that we are doing more than simply 'servicing' someone by engaging with them; that every small incident and interaction is part of a bigger picture that we can create together.

> When we first set up our joint peer supervision group, we agreed that one of the members would lead the group, as the 'trainer'. We omitted to agree a time to review this decision.
>
> One day, after a considerable number of sessions, we realised that we had made her 'mum', the Parent of the group! We were waiting for her to build the agenda, call us to time and lead the feedback. We were all contributing to the work, but we had subtly allowed a degree of passivity to become part of the way in which we participated.

By behaving in this way we discounted our own considerable individual and collective capabilities, so we gained less value from the process. In addition, we were diminishing the value to our colleague of the time she spent with us – we weren't fully participating in the contract for mutual learning we had intended to establish. The relationship between the 'leader' and the rest of the group was at risk of becoming cosy or co-dependent because everyone was slipping into familiar roles – one member being 'responsible', the rest 'followers'. Maybe these were personal narratives from our pasts, but they weren't needed in the current situation.

We were able to halt this slide and jointly challenge ourselves to re-contract. But it would have been so easy to miss!

To understand how easily such situations can happen, let's look at the way we make meaning and how we acquire our personal narratives – in TA language, our life-script.

Stories and life-scripts

> Those who do not have power over the stories that dominate their lives – the power to retell them, rethink them, deconstruct them, joke about them, and change them as times change – truly are powerless because they cannot think new thoughts.[2]

Stories make the world: we acquire verbal language as children; we develop metaphors to describe ourselves; these become the stories that reflect our individual world as we are experiencing it. Later we turn them into a general theory – our life-script, or 'psychological life-plan', creating our own explanatory narrative which gives meaning to the past, provides a problem-solving blueprint for the present and predicts the future.

What stories we choose to tell, and how we choose to tell them, depends on our culture. If our language and culture emphasises separateness, non-connectedness, objectification, then our stories will do the same. If our culture values connection and belonging, so will our stories.

We can say that, sometime around the age of three to seven years, everyone creates a meaning-making story about themselves and their place in the world. This is the Identity stage (see the cycle diagram in Chapter 2), where we arrive at a picture of who we are in our family and social group. This story, or life-script,[3] will be flexible. It will change as information is gathered and considered, sometimes as the result of significant and unexpected events, sometimes by refreshing earlier beliefs. Some people, though not all, include in this story decisions which may seriously damage their health; but their story will also include beliefs and strategies that promote survival and keep the little person safe, give a sense of self and a capacity for social interaction.

Included in the beliefs about ourselves, other people and the world that form part of our individual life-script, will be some about learning: our own ability, how others do or don't support us, where we place ourselves in a learning hierarchy.

Others will be about our own capacity – we're clever, slow, can think on our feet, can't understand – they will often be drawn from ideas we have absorbed as metaphors: learning is 'an uphill struggle' or, 'knowledge is power'.

As we encounter one another, our stories intersect; the meaning we have created for ourselves about ourselves and others changes, grows and gets challenged – and so evolves into a different story. With a bit of luck, this will be a mutual process transforming teachers' scripts as well as learners' (supervisors' as well as supervisees'). If our learning and our script are intertwined, each fresh learning event is a chance for us to re-do the meaning we give to our encounters. Arriving at a new theory, whether as an external exercise or an internal change in thinking or feeling, follows from re-creating meaning. Supervision is about changing the story – the story we tell and the story we don't tell.

> Some clients hook into Mary's need (as both coach and supervisor) to save them from themselves, from wasting their talent, from destroying their health or what is best in them.
>
> This is not a hero complex on Mary's part, it's about her embedded learning that 'Making it OK for the other' – particularly a talented, charismatic, energetic and fun other – is the safest way for her to look after herself in their presence. And these others, beneath their charisma, always make it clear to her that they are fundamentally fragile; she is the one they can trust and be vulnerable with; only she can make them feel safe.
>
> Mary was not happy with how she felt after working with this sort of client, and frequently brought to supervision her issues with the two she found particularly irksome. But it was only when she finally got utterly fed up with her own part in this, embarrassed at bringing it to supervision yet again, and was very directly challenged by members of the group, that she stopped trying to 'manage' her clients, their time, and the work they were doing – or not doing – with her. She stopped trying to save them from themselves.
>
> As she changed her thinking and attitude to her clients, they changed too. They took more initiative, showed up, shared more and developed more – were free to be themselves.
>
> Once she was aware of her own part in this struggle, she could behave differently when with them; she could hold herself – and them – to the belief that they were OK, that they could own their own decisions about how to live and work. Together with her colleagues in the group, Mary began to recognise the power of story-telling, and of the re-telling of the story.

What is going on when a coach keeps bringing what seems to be the same story to supervision? What is happening when a supervisor keeps telling themselves the same story about their supervisees or their clients? And how might we finally 're-story the story' in a restorative way?

When we hear familiar stories in supervision, we begin to notice how they develop and change in the telling. Now we can ask ourselves:

- Why does this story keep being told?
- What is the unmet need – is it perhaps, finally to be heard?
- If so, what will tell the story-teller they really are being heard?
- Are there certain consistent themes?
- What changes in the re-telling – the hero, the locus of control, the emotion, the ending?
- Are there archetypes emerging?
- What is the impact on us, as supervisor: do we find this disturbing, boring, or irritating?
- Are we starting to create our own story about (or for) this supervisee – and is it a helpful one?

Script and the learning cycle

Let your mind go back to a recent piece of supervision or, if you prefer, a coaching session – or even a recent time when you were the supervisee. Now review your experience:

Tell yourself the story of what happened – what 'problem' or puzzlement was described; what the other person said; what was said in response.

Then begin to review your feelings at the time – how was it for you:

- What significance did or does it have for you?
- What did you think and feel before, during and after the experience in question?
- What thoughts and feelings were brought about in the session, whether or not you were the 'subject', as the experience was discussed?

As you reflect, what ideas emerge: about yourself; the other person; how the incident relates to what you already know or are learning; do any models come to mind that illuminate what happened; or do you have a new idea to make sense of it?

Stay with that for a moment: what meaning can you take from – or create for – the situation now?

Now move on to think through the implications for the future: what have you learnt that might make a difference next time a similar situation occurs; what might you do differently; how will you embed the new decision or insight?

The experiential learning cycle

What you have just been doing in that exercise was to use a development of experiential learning, known as the learning cycle,[4] to review an experience of coaching or supervision. It may have been a familiar experience that you looked at; it probably was, because these familiar situations where we feel stuck or unable to move on are typically the issues we bring to supervision.

Many people have encountered the learning cycle as a model for training (Figure 4.1), but it is much more than this; it is an example of a major process of human adaptation – the way we 'get on' in the world.

This may be best known to us through the learning cycle, but essentially the same process underpins all science and art, and it is how, as babies and children, we grow, develop and learn.[5] What underlies all these scenarios is that we look

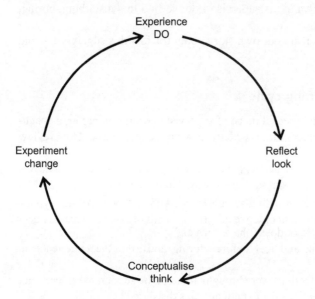

Figure 4.1   Experiential learning cycle.

Source: Napper and Newton 2014, 1:6.

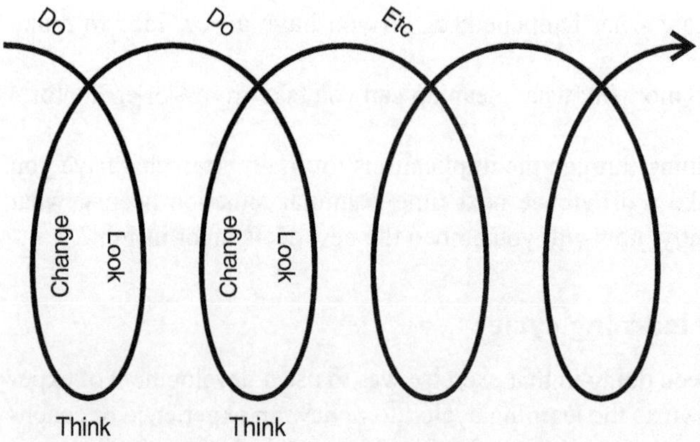

Figure 4.2   The learning spiral.

Source: Napper and Newton 2014, 1:6.

at what happened, think what it might mean, plan on that basis, see what happens now, adjust the theory – and all of that in an ongoing spiral.

This may not be the way that 'we think we think' about our everyday experiences, but if you pause to look back over the last few months, examples will begin to appear: learning something new to you, or solving something that's been a problem for you.

People learn most effectively when an experience can be considered, related to their established concepts, and a new action decided upon. This is how 'real' learning takes place: our behaviour changes as a result of reflecting on a specific experience and drawing conclusions about it.

And, of course, changed behaviour results in a new experience – and so the cycle starts again. More accurately, it becomes a spiral where each loop forms a further stage in the learning process of 'Do' (something), 'Look' (at what happened), 'Think' (about the implications) and 'Change' (what you do next time) (see Figure 4.2).

The learning cycle (or learning spiral) is the process by which we construct our stories (Figure 4.3). It's also a way of viewing script formation as a series of 'learning experiments' that accumulate to become our personal theories about ourselves and our world.[6]

Like a scientist, we consider data, devise experiments and test our hypotheses. Our life-script is the outcome we construct – and, of course, what has been constructed can also be de-constructed or re-constructed. We really can 'change reality by re-describing it'.[7]

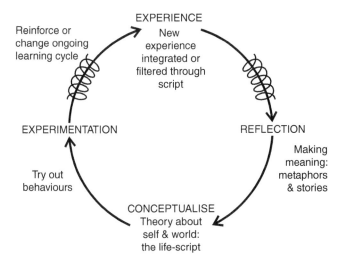

Figure 4.3   Script formation and the learning cycle.

Source: Adapted from Newton 2006, p. 191.

Experiential learning and the brain

This model of learning has been taken up by Professor James Zull, who studies innovation in teaching and education alongside biology and biochemistry.[8] Mapping the learning cycle onto the different areas of brain activity associated with stages of learning, he identifies a line of transformation between the parietal and frontal lobes where a change takes place from accepting and storing information into making our own unique use of it (Figure 4.4).

This can also be thought of as a position on the learning cycle between reflection and conceptualisation, where our sense of meaning turns into the creating of something new.

We use symbolisation and metaphor to explain to ourselves and others our understanding of our own understanding – our metacognition or mentalising. This active, aware engagement is a form of deep learning; it is a very pleasant experience, full of endorphins: we find joy in our discoveries and our actions.

Relational learning

The way most of us learn best is in relationship. Even if we're learning from a book, someone has created it, and in effect we are listening to their voice as we read and make our comments or develop the ideas.

Supervision is a place where authentic learning happens. Adult learning is most effective when it is based on experience (experiential learning) and is co-creative (in a two-person or multi-person setting).

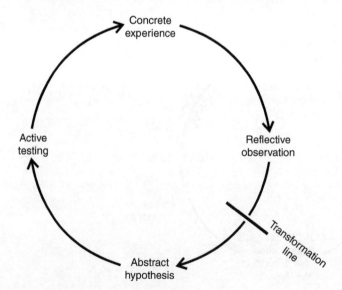

Figure 4.4   The transformation line.

Source: Zull 2002.

As part of the move towards more mutual and empathic approaches in all kinds of people-work (known as 'the relational turn'), there is a particular way of thinking which we call 'relational learning'. This has some indicators[9]:

The centrality of connection – the humanistic perspective we take from Carl Rogers and others, placing the learner-teacher relationship at the centre.[10] As Rogers suggests, the learning climate involves an acceptance of and caring for the learner as a separate person with permission to have her or his own feelings and experiences and to find her or his own meanings in them.

The significance of experience – offering relational experiences that both embody and enact for the learner meanings different from those that previous relationships might have, can be restorative, especially if they have felt judged and need a new experience of equality and respect:

> I really enjoyed the assessment. The reflection after the session created a great learning opportunity. I could analyse and voice what I did and why, what was my thinking, what choices did I see. The assessors' questions raised my awareness even more. They were respectful and curious about my thinking. Their feedback was constructive and based on evidence. I had the impression that during the hour of the assessment I learned as much as during a whole module.[11]

Subjectivity and inter-subjectivity – real learning happens through a 'disorienting dilemma' that leads to a change in self-perception; a challenge to some aspect of one's identity causes a change in the frame of reference. As well as being engaged in the learnings of the learner, the teacher will be creating new learnings for themselves.

> Hari believed he couldn't write so when a course he was keen to complete included a written assignment he refused to think about it until the deadline was approaching – and then said he couldn't fulfil the requirement.
>
> However, he did agree to explore his block with the tutor, who invited him to talk to her about what he could do. Hari admitted he had loads of ideas about the topic of the assignment, and could explain them verbally. After some further exploration, he agreed to be interviewed by his tutor and for their dialogue to be recorded.
>
> As he later transcribed the recording, Hari realised that he could write – if he did it his own way and not the way he had been expected to at school.
>
> He passed the assignment. He also discovered that he enjoyed it!

Engagement – when we talk and work together, questions of common concern come to the fore and are discussed as a joint enterprise. This is the two-person model.

Unconscious patterns – just like conscious patterns, relate to the cultural dimension. Our deeply held beliefs, our gender and our family, social and cultural scripting all have an impact, and have different ways of becoming manifest.

The functioning and changing adult/Adult – the supervisee is seen as, and is treated very much as, an adult capable of a reciprocal and mutual (albeit asymmetrical) relationship with the supervisor, and so the relationship promotes the 'expansion of the Adult'.

Curiosity, criticism and creativity – very early in life we begin to use a problem-solving investigative process: babies, toddlers and small children are just like little scientists; they make experiments, look at what happens and try again. This can be fun as well as instructive: we play in order to work out what's really going on; which may be why, as adults, we sometimes seek out experiences where we will certainly make mistakes, such as starting a new career – or even getting supervision.

Uncertainty – starting with an invitation to decide what we want and how we will find it is a scary thing: dependency is confronted, but then as possibilities open up there is a sense of liberation and a shared ownership of the new learning.

Using script, learning cycle and story in supervision

The learning cycle in supervision

Each problem or 'piece' brought to supervision provides an example. The supervision session is a forum in which the reflective process can take place; it may be extensive and include information-giving, question-posing, comparisons with other situations, exploration of personal process and emotional experience. There will be opportunities for considering familiar ways of working and exploring new ones.

Out of this 'thick description'[12] new meaning begins to emerge. This is the point at which practice and theory come together: theory informs the experience and the experience offers an opportunity for adjusting theory.

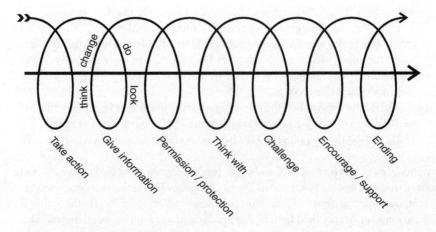

Figure 4.5   Developmental processes.

From this discussion, the supervisee can devise fresh plans for action in the future. These will feed in to their future experiences with the client (and similar experiences with other clients). Figure 4.5 shows the continuum of possible interventions by the supervisor combined with the learning spiral. As the supervisee's work is continually informed and updated by reflection and the resulting changes in practice, they move along the continuum growing in competence and confidence.

Stories and storyboards

A storyboard[13] maps out a story through its main ideas and principal characters. It is a method for developing plot, much used in film, television and advertising, and has a lot in common with the process of writing we described in the reflections. Based on the work of Mooli Lahad, it is a creative and imaginative way to free up supervisees' thinking. Table 4.1 shows an example.

> Imagine watching a film: it begins with scenes that tell us something about where and when the action is set, and then it moves in to a closer view of place and circumstance. This is when someone appears in the scene and something begins to happen.
>
> By now we begin to have an idea of what this story will be about, but it really becomes a story when things begin to go wrong: the rest of the plot is the resolution, with or without help from other characters, and then the film ends with a 'takeaway' – something learnt or understood that we didn't know before.

Telling a story this way in supervision can be a way of unblocking recurring 'stuckness' and perhaps showing how the supervisee's beliefs intrude on the work. The exercise can also be a beautiful and enlightening means of reviewing your supervision partnership. We also use storyboards in workshops and reviews with supervisors to support reflection on their own growth over a certain time.

The template has nine elements and in each one you can draw, or write a piece of the story or combine the two. Like a fairy tale, it starts with a landscape; then it focuses on something within the landscape – a dwelling; then a character; then a 'situation'. It ends with resolution and learning.

Taking an example from the coaching world, the landscape might be an organisation that the coach works in, with its own distinctive culture and ways of operating. Within that, the dwelling could be a group or team the coach is working with. The character may be the coach as he brings something to supervision, and the challenge the general context of that problem or issue. Who or what are the helpers, what exactly the difficulty is, and how it will be overcome, will be revealed in the process of the supervision.

Table 4.1 Storyboard template

LANDSCAPE	DWELLING	CHARACTER
What was the general context?	The specific context or situation?	Who is the key person or hero of the story?
CHALLENGE	HELPER	DIFFICULTY
What happened?	Who gave support or assistance?	What created the problem or stuckness?
SOLUTION	LEARNING	FUTURE
How did/will you overcome it?	What does this tell you that is new or reinforced?	What will you take away to use in other stories?

Creating the environment for learning

What makes the difference between an indifferent or adequate experience in supervision and one that feels important, integrated and liberating – and produces those endorphins?

We all know what makes a good learning experience: clear contracting with attention to the psychological level; a safe space through the balancing of challenge and support; all egostates engaged; experience and reflection as well as theory and practice. And we all know that sometimes a session will go well, sometimes less well, sometimes disastrously. And just sometimes there is a very special feel to it that is hard to identify – but everyone there knows that they have changed and that real learning has happened.

'The educator as cultivator' is a metaphor created by Giles Barrow[14]: a positive parental role that means taking care of the soil like a gardener, allowing things to happen in their own time, and acting swiftly if something starts to go wrong.

The same may be said of a supervisor: establishing trust with an individual or within a group – modelling potency, permission and protection – is a crucial role. Together with the creation of a healthy learning climate that demonstrates acceptance and permission, it provides the soil.

The quality of attention that shows a real awareness of each person as they are in the here-and-now, which holds the space, prompts authentic interactions and allows each person to grow at their own pace, is the job of a cultivator.

What all this tells us is that relationship and contact is fundamental to learning. Our development and our preferences for one way of life over another are derived from interaction with our social environment, they are not 'decided' or 'programmed' by it. Learning is the process of creating knowledge: it results from the transaction between social knowledge and personal knowledge – it is not a linear acquisition of information. Human beings are learners and meaning-makers, we create our world through stories that both reflect and contribute to the dynamic flow of our lives.

The script system in supervision

A new model from a relational TA perspective looks at 'supervision in action' in order to describe and diagram this inter-subjective process[15]:

The diagram shows four quadrants, which represent stages in the formation and maintenance of the personal script:

- A. Experiences from the past apparently repeated in present interpersonal dynamics.
- B. The meaning we make from this, and the stories we create about 'how the world is'.
- C. The patterns of thinking and feeling we derive from our meaning-making.
- D. The way we behave and act in the world based on those patterns.

This model is both a 'snapshot' of script and a way of understanding what is happening in the moment; we can use it to clarify the boundary between the here-and-now supervision and the personal issues which may be generating difficulties for the coach.

The 'A' and 'B' sections may be in the realm of therapy; however, an aware-ness of internal experience is crucial in effective supervision, and we have already discussed the power of the supervisor's own use of self, the value of connecting with apparently irrational sensations and feelings, which can provide so much information in the work. This 'coming together' is the area of the relational field, an image of the inter-subjective experience of learning.

As coaches develop, they change their sense of themselves as coaches – and the same goes for supervisors. Looking at the diagram, this involves the 're-doing' of meaning (B) – new interpretations of experiences that lead to new decisions and actions. This openness to change and the move into new thinking and feel-ing corresponds to Zull's 'transformation line', or in TA language a re-writing of script – for all participants.

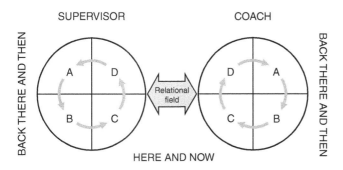

Figure 4.6 The relational field in supervision.

Source: Based on Sills and Mazzetti 2009.

The effect of the relational field, where we meet one another through our external actions and our internal thinking patterns, is transferred into our personal meaning-making and enables us to see things afresh. This is what we can call 'relational learning'.

The diagram in Figure 4.6 allows an appreciation of the process at work in transformational learning: when we encounter each other, first 'D' and then 'C' interact – this is the relational field, working with the interpersonal dynamics of both partners. 'B' and 'A' are 'back there and then' in the past, beyond the boundary of a learning relationship, but they profoundly affect what happens in the here-and-now.

However, by interrogating the here-and-now occurrence for all participants we can start to bring 'B' into the light – though not necessarily into conscious awareness. What happens next is often a significant process of transformation: we can change the meaning we give to our experience. This 're-doing' is real learning, learning through lived-out experience, and it is mutual: all involved will be affected. Shifting fragments re-align in a new pattern and a new story emerges; attitudes, beliefs and decisions about the self-in-learning are updated.

> Letting go of my old awareness of who I am
> Supposed to be and embracing who I am
> Who am I?[16]

A participant in a recent workshop for supervisors expressed her response in this way:

> This model made clear to me for the first time the ways in which I can work with script in supervision. The correlation of experience and making meaning (A and B) with the past and thinking/feeling and behaviour (C and D) with the present helps me to be very clear about where the script becomes useful rather than destructive. As I turn to face my supervisee, we meet in the present where the work is co-creating a new meaning for both of us. The work we are doing is internal, reflective work, facilitated by the supervisor. The supervisor acknowledges that the work is mutual, my script now interacting with her script, within the contracted boundary of supervision, in order to change behaviour mainly for the supervisee, but acknowledging the change effected in me as supervisor by this encounter. It helped me to move from doing supervision to being a supervisor.[17]

The following story illustrates how this can be experienced by a supervisee:

Jack's story

Jack had retired from his coaching practice but wanted to continue to do some work as a coach in the community he lived in. A friend, Ava, asked if he would support her as she went through expanding and re-focussing her business. This was exactly the work Jack excelled at and he gladly agreed. They would 'boundary' the time, keeping it separate from family socialising.

All went well until Ava decided that she wanted to make some radical changes in the way she and her family lived. From then on, Jack and Ava's intended-to-be business coaching sessions turned into personal coaching as Ava and her family became embroiled in a series of decisions that were complicated and disruptive. Of course, this wasn't the first time in Jack's coaching career that he had worked with a client on a family issue.

However, Jack's problem was that he had his own opinions on the decision and the way Ava was approaching it. How was he going to keep himself out of it when he cared about the whole family? As Ava's coach, he was finding it hard to stay in that role and not be the worried friend. Outside the sessions he found himself 'siding' with others, worrying about the rest of her family and assuming it would all end in disaster!

He realised he couldn't go on doing this and took it to supervision to work out what it was all about for him. He realised that he was furious at the destruction of his fantasy of them as a smoothly functioning and serenely happy family – the family he wanted them to be. He was angry that they were doing things he had never been allowed to do, and was fearful of the family breaking up.

Two things were apparent: the professional distance of their relationship had become distorted, and his own perspective had been created in a dysfunctional family.

But Ava and her family were not his family! Once he understood what he was bringing into the coaching sessions, he was able to restore the distance between them, and support her in finding her own way and making her own decisions.

He also was able to share his concerns and use his coaching skills to challenge her appropriately on her motivation. And he could own his own sadness at the impact this had on him.

Updating our stories

Supervisor and coach are engaged together in a co-creative process; re-writing, or re-deciding, part of their personal narratives.

It is through you
I see me
And so you see more of you.[18]

We have all arrived at decisions about who we are and how OK we are. These decisions, along with the beliefs we have arrived at about how the world works, form our personal story or life-script – our childhood meaning-making; these may include some parts that are limiting or even harmful. Every time we challenge our limiting beliefs, recognise a game we play and decide to do something different or action OK-OK transactions, we are writing part of a healthier story for ourselves.

> The great advantage of having told a story about the world is realising that we can tell a better one; rich with better ideas, better possibilities – even perhaps better people.[19]

Like our original story-making, we do this in relationship, not alone.

Notes

1 Clark, A., *Guardian* review, p. 3, 11 March 2017, 'Writers Unite! The return of the protest novel'.
2 Rushdie, S., 'Excerpts From Rushdie's Address: 1,000 days "trapped inside a metaphor"', *New York Times*, 12 December 1991, p. 480.
3 *Life-script(script)*: a set of beliefs and decisions made in childhood which continue to influence a person's life. Scripts include both self-limiting and self-protective beliefs and decisions; they can be updated as a person takes in new information, and they can be changed.
4 Experiential learning, and the learning cycle, in the form that most people think about them today, were described by David Kolb in the 1980s. These ideas have become the underpinning of much adult education as well as training courses, and a model for all learning to balance the traditional modes of 'information giving' schooling. Kolb's classic work also details research on learning style and career choices, the psychology of learning and the adaptive process, and defines learning as 'the creation of knowledge by the transformation of experience'.
5 Alison Gopnik and her colleagues in Berkeley, California, describe babies as 'little scientists' making experiments and learning from the results. Their utterly fascinating book, *The Scientist in the Crib* (or *How Babies Think* in the UK edition) is a significant contribution to child development literature – and is also easy to read.
6 Life-script formation can be understood as a series of learning cycles – in summary:

- Script formation, reinforcement and updating can be seen as a series of learning cycles, continually re-creating our life-narrative.
- The learning cycle provides a model for understanding childhood learning and script development in childhood.
- It also provides a model for understanding the process of changing or updating script throughout life.
- This is a constant and inevitable process, part of human adaptation.
- Construction, deconstruction and reconstruction can be perceived as reflection on experience, conceptualisation and experimentation.

7 The idea that we change reality by re-describing it is taken from the work of Don Cupitt, in particular his writing on ethics.
8 Research on neuroscience and learning is beginning to produce evidence that this way of thinking about learning has a physical base in brain activity. James Zull began this work when he took on, as a university professor in the USA, a project to improve teaching and learning for students. Much more can be found in *The Art of Changing the Brain: Enriching the practice of teaching by exploring the biology of learning* (2002) where he invites teachers to accompany him in his exploration of what we know about the brain and how this knowledge can influence teaching practice.

9 These eight indicators of a relational approach in therapy were suggested by Fowlie and Sills in *Relational Transactional Analysis* (2011). A discussion of how they connect to current ideas of adult learning can be found in L'AT Relationelle dans l'education, *Actualites en Analyse Transactionelle,* 141, Newton 2012.

10 Paolo Freire, Carl Rogers and Jack Mezirow are key thinkers in the field of radical education and experiential learning. Rogers and Freire, writing around the same time in the 1960s and 1970s, both made the learner, rather than the subject, the focus of learning and saw the teacher as one who creates an environment in which learning can happen, not as a dispenser of knowledge. Mezirow's idea of transformative learning includes the psychological dimension of 'change in understanding of the self'.

11 Thanks to Leda Turai for this reflection on her experience (personal communication 2011).

12 *A thick description* of a human behaviour explains not just the behaviour itself but its context as well, so that it can become meaningful to an outsider.

13 Mooli Lahad encourages the use of stories, drawing, letter-writing and many other 'right-brain' ideas to develop creativity in supervisees, a therapeutic process for them and for their clients.

14 Barrow developed this idea in an article 'Educator as Cultivator' (2011), where he considers the integration of traditional farming principles into the context of learning.

15 The model that describes the 'here and now' and 'back there and then' aspects of supervision comes from the work of Charlotte Sills and Marco Mazzetti in an article published in 2009. Their model can also be used to analyse the coaching relationship. Their aim is to give visual substance and impact to the concept of the relational field and its connection to personal script.

16 Thanks to Thabiso Baloyi, from a workshop for coach supervisors, Cape Town, April 2015.

17 Thanks to Diane Clutterbuck for permission to include this extract from her notes on a supervision workshop 2011.

18 Thanks to Sally Brazier, from a workshop for coach supervisors, Cape Town, April 2015.

19 The quotation at the end of this chapter is from *Being Wrong* by Kathryn Schulz. She describes what she calls the meta-mistake of *being wrong about being wrong* – when our desire to be right, as individuals or as social groups, prevents us from seeing that sometimes being wrong or making mistakes is an essential part of learning, p. 339.

Chapter 5

Creating effective contracts
Empathy and rigour

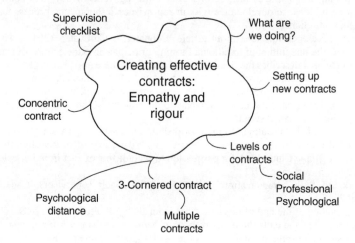

The supervisor was rigorous. She identified the focus for the session and quickly eliminated any need to focus on the 'you', 'they' or 'it'. She did this compassionately and ruthlessly, for example: 'That's really interesting and it's not what we are here to talk about' and, 'It doesn't sound like this is the nub of the issue. Would you agree?'

Instead of the content of the session, contracting became the focal point for the majority of the audience. We could see the importance of clarifying the focus of a supervision or coaching session.[1]

What is the contract?

What are we doing and why are we doing it? The question we ask most frequently in supervision is, 'What is the contract?', which generally causes recognition of what is going wrong – and how it can be put right.

We are not used to negotiating our relationships in detail, and certainly not early on or repeatedly over time. We like to ease into a relationship; we unintentionally bring with us our old and unexpressed hopes that we can 'get this one right', that nothing can go wrong, that, somehow, we'll just make it work. But, when eyeballed harshly, reality reminds us that this is rarely so! How many truly vulnerable, open, creative or productive relationships have lasted over time on the basis that they 'just happened to happen'?

In any meeting of two or more people (and even of self with one's self) there is always a contract[2] – whether it is declared or not. And there is always a contract at the psychological level; we may call this level 'expectations' or 'assumptions'. Later on, when things do not seem to be going well, they will typically be expressed as, 'I always thought … I assumed … I really needed / wanted / expected you to …'.

Contracting sometimes feels 'clunky', awkward, or even not respectful; the truth is that, no matter how long we have been doing the work, there will always be times when this will be the case. And, yet, when supervisors get together to talk about their work, we often hear them saying, 'If we were taught just one thing it would have to be contracting', 'The contract is the work' or even, 'Whatever the question, the answer is to look at the contract'.

Without a contract, we are embarking on a significant and potentially scary journey on an open sea without a rubber ring – let alone a boat – and the first big wave is going to sink us.

> Jade was one of the supervisors working with a group of coaches in training. At their first meeting she asked each of them to report on where they were with their clients, and what they were bringing to supervision. Some said they had not done any coaching; none had been keeping their reflective journal; all seemed resentful at having to be there. One student was willing to bring a piece of work to supervision, and it rapidly became clear that the difficulty in the coaching was a lack of a contract between coach and client.
>
> This provoked a group discussion about contracting. The view expressed by a number of the students was encapsulated by one who said, 'Well, coaching's just all about listening isn't it? We need to let the client talk it out; they'll sort themselves. We're there to hold a caring space, contracting just makes the client feel really uncomfortable.'

Contracting is the place where we really start to recognise that this is a working relationship, a relationship which is about work, and in which work is done. In order for this to be successful, it is important that a contract is established that can contain all that may emerge in a way that is both safe and productive.

Later on we will look in detail at the structures and processes for creating and updating a living relational contract. We will discuss how the contract varies between different contexts and how the dual concepts of empathy and rigour always inform our approach. We will include one-to-one, three-way and multi-party contracts, levels of contracting (the social, professional and psychological) and ways of working with group and organisational contracts.

How we contract

The first question is, 'Why are we in this relationship? Why here and not somewhere else; why with me and not with another; what is it that we can do here for which this is the best place, or maybe the only place. How, explicitly, are we going to make this relationship serve its purpose?'

There are three key concepts that inform the contract and underpin the way we think about the supervision relationship:

- How do we establish good contact between us?
- How do we ensure that we are working in a way that is rigorous?
- How do we ensure mutuality?

With this goes a deep respect for (and a willingness to understand) just how different each of us can be, and therefore a recognition that both of us will have to be honest about our own needs and start to recognise where they may come into conflict with the other's.

Establishing contact

How do we go about establishing contact ourselves?

> Left to myself, I will come straight into a meeting with whatever is in my head: I was mentoring on a training course and overnight I had processed something significant which had happened the day before. I bounced into the training room, met my colleague and immediately started to pour out all my new thoughts and understandings.
>
> When I finally paused for breath, he said, 'And good morning to you Hilary … did you have a pleasant evening … and how was your journey this morning? … mine was fine, but a bit wet,' and so on! He really needed contact before we started contracting for an important conversation.

Trudi has her own story:

> I remember working in an organisation where I and the person commissioning me were a good match – we both liked to start by having coffee and catching up before getting down to planning and scheduling. Having made that contact we then worked efficiently and well. Then she was replaced by someone with a very different attitude: as soon as I appeared we began to work – while I was thinking, 'Where's my coffee?'
>
> The next time I was to go to a planning meeting, I made sure to arrive early and have coffee with another colleague first!

So, when we began working together, we needed to understand how different our needs were and that this would be true each time we met afresh – and it needed to be understood and acted upon each time if we were to make the right connection to do our work together.

Rigour

This connects with knowing that there is a job to be done. It's not a chat with a friend, it's not just a warm bath of unconditional support, and neither is it an opportunity for someone to be managed or found out. It is a place where there is a structure and a purpose. Keeping the contract in mind, recognising that we are here for a purpose, maintains the rigour of the supervision session.

But we also need sensitivity and flexibility. The story at the start of this chapter is from notes a coach made on observing a contracting process. He saw it as 'compassionate and ruthless' – good observation of the intended empathy and rigour.

Mutuality

This is one outcome of empathic work and also brings us to the issue of expertise: is it the role of the supervisor to be the expert, to hand down wisdom and clearly communicate how to do it right? We don't think so; though it is reasonable to expect of the supervisor that they can be 'stronger and wiser in the moment'. The relationship will be equal and mutual – and also sometimes asymmetric.

There are other relationships which may be modelled differently (for example consulting or mentoring) but in supervision, unless both parties are willing to work in the territory of mutual vulnerability and courage, then work of real value cannot happen.

The supervisee is not a seeker but a co-learner, co-creating new wisdom from which both they and the supervisor benefit and grow. And this new wisdom becomes a resource which can be shared without attachment. But in order to arrive at this relational Nirvana, contracting has first to occur!

The contract is a reference point that can be returned to and renegotiated. The first step is always to clarify what the contract is, and to do this we need to establish some guidelines for each unique relationship.

Contracts at the start

This exercise, based on a solution-focus model,[3] gives a base for contract-making in beginning a new supervision partnership. Before using it with a new supervisee, you can ask yourself these questions (or go through them with a colleague):

- How do you learn? What is your learning style? How can I facilitate that?
- How will you know you are getting what you want from supervision?
- How will I know this supervision is useful to you?
- What might I do that would block your development?
- How will you let me know I need to be doing something different?
- What differences between us might impact on the process?
- What do I need to know about your way of working?
- How will you know you are moving forward?
- What kind of situations are you good at working with?

- What situations are tough for you?
- If I feel anxious about your work, how would you like us to handle that?
- How will we learn together?

The contract is the work

We often use this phrase, but what does it really mean?

On one of our courses we decided to make this live: one of us did a piece of work in front of the group in which the supervisor was required to spend the entire session simply getting clarity with the supervisee on the contract – for thirty minutes! Thirty minutes is quite often an entire session, or at least will cover one of the topics brought to supervision.

What happened? Firstly, great discomfort on both sides. But what followed was a fascinating piece of work. Everything was explored:

- What's the topic?
- Why are you bringing it here; why me; why is this the best place; is it the only place – why?
- Why now; what has brought it to the top of your list; have we had this one before – if so, was it the same, was it different; is it one-of-a-kind or a one-off?
- What really is the supervision question – the dilemma; what is it that needs to be resolved?
- How are we both feeling – is there anything uncomfortable about this topic for either of us?
- Is there anything you don't want to talk about in this session?
- What do you want from me?
- Where do you want to get to with this?
- What do you think might be the key issue here?
- Could you re-state the question?
- Why do you want us to work together on this?
- What thinking have you already done on this?

By the end of the contracting, the supervisee had got to a point of complete clarity on what specifically was the issue, why it had been troubling them, and what was the resolution – just by being really rigorous about the contract.

Levels of contract

Contracting happens at several levels[4]:

The social or administrative level

This concerns what the supervisor and supervisee will do together – how often they will meet; face-to-face, by phone or online; the overt agenda and purpose;

does the supervisee pay or their organisation, and how much; how many sessions and for how long each time.

It deals with the structure of the supervision sessions. Negotiating this is like constructing a framework from which supervision can start.

Together you decide:

- Frequency of contact.
- Time – will it be for an hour, or more, or less, or open-ended?
- Place – will you meet, talk by phone, use email or meet online?
- Access between agreed meetings – is this the only opportunity to talk and if not, what circumstances would bring about further contact? How will that be contracted for and paid for?
- Confidentiality – who knows what happens in this meeting?
- Recording – are you going to record and if yes, how are you going to do this and who keeps the record? How long will recordings be kept and who will hear them?
- Evaluation and review – when and how are these to happen? What will you do if either person wants to end the contract?

The professional level

The social contract implies a professional contract – how will we two (or more) work together; how will we relate; what competencies and experience do we each bring; is this an appropriate partnership or would another supervisor be more suited; how will we establish trust and purpose?

This is negotiated in order to agree working practice. If you don't take time to agree, you may be working to totally different expectations.

- Purpose – what is the main reason for the supervision?
- Aims – what do we both want to get from these sessions? Aims give a general and agreed idea of what the supervision is for.
- Objectives – specific goals and objectives can be set, overall and for each session, to focus the work.
- Methods – how is the session going to work? What supervision models will you use?
- Responsibilities of the supervisor – for example, being prepared, allocating time, facilitating the supervision process and being adequately trained.
- Responsibilities of the supervisee – for example, being prepared, being open to the supervision process, identifying and sharing developmental needs.
- Style of supervision – for example, formal or informal, a detailed analysis of coach's progress or a general overview; content or process led?
- Directing the session – does this come from the supervisee, the supervisor, or is it negotiated from meeting to meeting?

The psychological level

Beneath these two, there lies a further, hidden contract sometimes known as the psychological level. This is where outcomes are determined; it concerns the 'messages' about our beliefs and how we really see the supervision process which we hold in mind or on the edge of our awareness and unconsciously send to others: will I aim to get the supervisor on my side? Will I hold onto my unconscious belief that nothing can ever change? Am I out to prove that this won't work for me?

All these beliefs may be held by the supervisee, the supervisor ('Am I up to this?' or, 'How can I get them to use me again?') – or by a third party.

For the supervision to be successful, this hidden level needs to be addressed, perhaps by asking, 'What concerns do you have about supervision?', 'How will I know if this isn't working for you?', 'If we have a problem, how will we deal with it or recover from it?', 'What might I do or say that would damage our working together?' or, 'How might you sabotage your success?'

All these and similar questions help to bring any potential difficulties into the open, just as does clarity about the social and professional levels.

Good contracting takes account of this aspect of the supervision relationship, and so enhances:

- Awareness – what goes on in the interactions? Are they clear and straightforward or are there sometimes secret agendas?
- Openness – how will you address any difficulties or let each other know if the process isn't working?
- Autonomy – are coach and supervisor both taking their own responsibility? How will you address collusion or conflict?
- Flexibility – what options do you see for moving on, using a range of skills and keeping the supervision engaging?

These questions, used when first setting up a new supervisory relationship, are a way of getting to know each other and give a real sense of engaging in something together. We use them as a first session – exploring them is part of supervision: setting parameters, modelling good practice, paying attention to the personal needs and aptitudes of the supervisee. They help to bring more of the psychological level into awareness, and they need to be revisited at intervals to make sure we are not drifting into assumptions or complacency.

Although it can feel time-consuming, time spent on good contracting is never wasted. Through the process, all involved parties will know what we are here to do, trust each other to do it and work authentically towards real, testable outcomes – establishing the ground for effective supervision.

Of course, the psychological level of the contract may well be positive from the start, with everyone invested in success, but it still needs to be kept in awareness and included in reviews of your work.

Process contracting

Equally importantly, we don't want to give the impression that contracting is a bounded area of supervision that happens at the start and then only comes back into the session at the end. Ideally, it will permeate the pattern and flow of the work as a constant reference point.

Questions or interventions such as, 'Where are you now?', 'I have a sense that you are getting clearer', 'Is this the area you want to focus on?', 'Let's leave that aside for now – or do we need to re-contract?', will keep attention on 'What are we here for?' and allow that the answer might change as we go along. This is known as 'process contracting' and gives a flexibility and reciprocity to the work.

Extending the contract

Everything about the supervision contract also applies to the coach-client contract – the importance of the social or 'business' level, the need for established competence at the professional level and so on – but the supervision contract has a number of other strengths: it can address any uncertainties in the coach's contracting by identifying the parallel process and 'working back down the system'; it can shed light on what might be happening between coach and client or between client and colleagues or managers, or even how the client may be carrying the burden of a lack of healthy contracting in their organisation.

There is also something important about the way in which contracting is part of the infrastructure of coaching, and how supervision for coaches is a 'proper' profession. We need a conscious decision to work in a particular way, and to a particular outcome, in order to evidence what we are doing – and how we are making good use of people's time and money.

If we indulge in some sort of mystical thinking – that we might be restricting what we do by saying what we're thinking and what we want – we encourage our clients in dependency: we are waving the magic wand and implying they can't achieve their goals without us. Reluctance to contract thoroughly, early, and often, may indicate an unwillingness in the coach to allow the client to be uncomfortable, and in the supervisor to allow the supervisee to be uncomfortable – but it is structure that gives us the freedom to work on this very relational basis.

Ask yourself: what do I think I am actually doing when I raise awareness of the psychological level? And what are my beliefs about contracting when I'm working as a supervisor and when I'm working as a coach? What comes up for me?

This emphasis on the details of contracting may make it sound heavy and off-putting ('why can't we just get on with the work on the problem?'), but familiarity with the idea of effective contracting and regular use of the questions soon gets it into the muscle, so that making a proper contract for a piece of work – whether a one-off session or a long-term relationship – comes to feel grounded and purposeful.

In executive or organisational coaching the contract is often limited to a number of sessions, typically six to eight; and, while it may be extended, it is usually limited in duration.

The supervision contract is very different. The initial contract is often for six to twelve months, with a review after an agreed time; and it may then continue for years, reviewed annually. This happens both one-to-one and in groups. In all these contexts, we notice what happens in long-term and stable relationships. What changes; what becomes possible; how does the work evolve?

One of the most obvious and valuable developments is the increasing level of trust, safety and empathy that comes from working together over time in a contracted-for relationship. A portfolio of positive reference experiences is established and a useful level of history is held by the supervisor – which can help in spotting repeating patterns, and also in holding the trajectory of development, of positive change and success.

Over time, the parties to the relationship come to understand and tolerate each other's quirks and oddities but, because of the commitment to remain in relationship, they also need to look to themselves and understand why they are finding the other's behaviours, ways of thinking and emotions uncomfortable. In so many relationships, it's easy to walk away once things get difficult – but in the supervision relationship, a specific element of the contract acknowledges that learning to confront and negotiate a way through awkward times in the relationship is an opportunity for growth, enhancing the ability to do this in other, different, relationships.

Our experience has taught us that stability and longevity in supervision relationships, whether one-to-one or in groups, has enormous value – and contributes greatly to the development of the participants. Our professional world can seem a very small one, and the opportunities for embarrassment or shame rather great. Having somewhere to go, where one has a history of safety with challenge, is of immeasurable benefit to our ability to be effective in our work.

Three (or more) party contracting

Contracting is not only multi-level, it is also multi-faceted. Often, agreeing a new contract happens one-to-one between supervisor and coach; but there may be others involved in a wider contracting.

Fanita English first described the three-cornered contract[5] between the practitioner, the client and the organisation. She observed that in contracting with training groups there was usually a sense of a hidden influence from outside the room, the 'Big Powers' who had set up the training.

This influence might lead to fantasies about the role of the trainer or the Big Powers' intentions. Contracting between all three – and sharing the results – makes for more effective and healthier training events.

We can apply this idea to the supervisor, the coach and the agency/associateship/employing organisation (Figure 5.1).

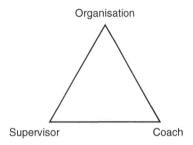

Figure 5.1   The three-cornered contract.

Source: Based on English 1975.

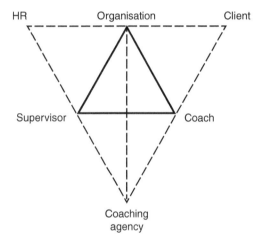

Figure 5.2   Multiple contracts.

Often, there will be yet further parties and sub-parties to the contract. An individual coach may have implicit contracts with a manager, human resources, associates, or the partnership that employs them; the organisation may be part of a group committed to coaching for everyone, and so on (Figure 5.2).

Coaching can become so focused on the client's agenda that the others involved – the employing organisation for instance – are forgotten. I recall asking a coach who was enthusing about their client's creativity and talent, and about how they were planning to leave their employer: 'Who's paying you?'

Awareness of all these influencing relationships, their potential impact on the contract between coach and client, and how to draw them out visually is a great tool at the start of a supervision piece. Many coaches, at the start of a new coaching relationship, take part in three-way meetings with the client and their manager. If the coach knows the three (or more) cornered contract model and uses it as a thinking framework in preparing for the meeting, while it is happening and for reflection afterwards, it makes for clarity in the coaching relationship.

Psychological distance

Clear contracting implies an equal OK-OK connection between client, coach, supervisor and the organisation. In the triangle in Figure 5.1, the distance between the three parties is perceived as equal, contracts and expectations are clear on all sides, and there is clear role-definition for everyone. It implies that all partners are open, willing to cooperate, and have no hidden agendas.

Most often, this is the result of extensive negotiation and preparation among the parties; sharing information, clarifying each contract and involving the client group in preliminaries, to ensure effective outcome-oriented work.

If the triangle doesn't feel equilateral, and the relationships don't feel well-contracted in all directions, the contract has become skewed (due, perhaps, to the psychological level not being sufficiently addressed). The equilateral triangle represents a situation where all expectations and responsibilities are clear; if it becomes distorted so that some parties are psychologically closer and others more distant, the supervisor can ask, 'What do you need to do to get the contract back to a healthy place?'

In Figure 5.3, we show the various distortions that can occur.[6] Recognising them (and the collusion they indicate), clarifies who needs to do what. This will help to get back to a balanced triangle and re-clarify the three-way contract.

a   This pattern occurs when supervisor and coach feel they are on the same wavelength but distant from the Big Powers (whoever they may be), due to their lack of involvement or a shared mistrust of them by supervisor and coach. The supervisor may be 'Rescuing' the coach or colluding in their mistrust, and together they may 'blame the boss'.

b   Here, the Big Powers and the supervisor may be clear about their goals, but have not consulted the coach – who may then be seen by them as deviant and unreceptive. This can happen when the supervisor identifies with the Big Powers, and is then perceived as Persecuting by the coach, who becomes passive and unwilling to engage.

c   The supervisor here is perceived as an outsider by both the Big Powers and the coach, and so feels isolated and in 'Victim'. This can happen when the supervisor is brought in for appearances' sake, or to comply with a code of practice, but with no real buy-in; or when Big Powers and coach share a strong corporate culture that believes, 'We don't need any help round here.'

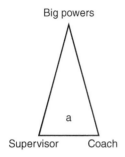

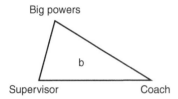

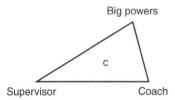

Figure 5.3   Psychological distance.
Source: Based on Micholt 1992.

Interventions to prevent distortions and maintain an equal contract can be initiated through:

- making the process transparent – even perhaps teaching the three-cornered contract;
- clarifying roles, expectations, needs and values;
- acknowledging power structures;
- identifying options for change.

Impact and dynamics in a supervision group

In any group, the contract will be affected by the dynamics between its members. This story illustrates some of the pitfalls – and also some of the plusses – of asking ourselves, 'What are we here to do?'

Peter had a talent for attracting interesting and talented people to work with him. A small group of these got together at his suggestion and asked Ryan to run a supervision group for them.

At the start, the only relationship all of them shared was with Peter. Although the others were by no means new to coaching, Peter was the most experienced coach in the group. He was always very clear about how the group needed to work – for him: his was the dominant voice in organising where, when, and how frequently they would be meeting.

He then began to let them know that he would not be present for some of the meetings and someone else would have to organise them. He started to forget the dates and times of meetings, book other activities so that he had to arrive late or leave early, or just not come at all!

The rest of the group increasingly resented this, though it took a long time for them to raise the issue.

At one session Peter had forgotten to attend, the group decided they'd like to make overt their commitment to each other and to the work of the supervision group. They would book meetings at regular intervals for the whole of the following year and each pay an equal share of the annual fees.

Dates were booked then and there – and they told Peter their decision later on. He was not happy; he was not willing to commit financially, logistically or emotionally to a year up-front. He rang Ryan to tell him privately that he was getting bored with the work in the group and didn't feel he was learning anything – and in fact was planning to drop out. In the meantime the rest of the group had decided that they weren't willing to continue working with Peter due to what they felt was his lack of commitment.

Forward to nearly a year later. The group (minus Peter) are all attending regularly, doing work of real depth and developing as coaches. They are co-coaching each other and becoming increasingly connected.

One of the group said, 'Since we made our commitment to each other explicit, the depth, trust and consistency of our relationships has really accelerated. We're dealing with really challenging stuff and growing so much more, and more quickly – and we're doing it together!'

And here is a look at how the story might have been, from the point of view of psychological distance, and a cleaner contract created:

Initially, Peter seemed very collaborative in contracting for how the group would be, but he rapidly initiated a pattern of taking over and coaching whilst giving feed-back.

At a meeting when Peter was absent, one of the members made a sarcastic – and funny – remark about his absence. It became clear from unspoken signals that conversations had been going on about Peter.

Ryan asked if there was something that they wanted to talk about, here in the group. They did. While he held the space, but stayed out of the debate, the group began to share their thoughts and feelings about their work together – how it had been and how they wanted it to be. When Ryan asked if there was something they wanted to do about how they felt, they began to make plans as in the story above and took responsibility for telling Peter about their decisions.

Staying neutral and remembering that everyone was party to the contract was crucial. Looking again at Figure 5.3:

- If Ryan had got too involved in this, he might have 'Rescued' the group by siding with them against Peter (triangle a), blaming him and maybe offering to talk to him on the group's behalf.
- Or else (triangle b), when Peter called him he could have derided the group's competence and plotted with him to coach rather than supervise the rest of the group, and thus criticise their work. Most likely this would have prompted them all to leave, proving that Peter was right all along.
- Or again (triangle c), he could have isolated himself by declaring that Peter had set up the group and therefore they should go along with his vision – and thus get out of an uncomfortable situation without solving anything.

The contract with the organisation matters as much as the contract with the coach. In the next chapter we will look at ethics and boundaries and how these can affect – and are affected by – transparency, organisational relationships, and culture.

Concentric contracting

New supervisors sometimes feel constrained by the contracting process and think they can't move on in the supervision until the contract is watertight; but contracting is really a process that flows through the session and can be changed, re-contracted and readjusted as issues emerge and difficulties are illuminated.

This can feel like 'going down and coming back up again' as the psychological level is made apparent and produces changes in behaviour both in and outside the room.

Looking at the full picture we can imagine three concentric circles (Figure 5.4):

- The outer represents the 'container' of the overall contract – 'What is this about?'
- The next circle is the relational contract. It is here that the quality, focus and outcome are determined – this is the psychological contract.
- The inner circle is the actual content, the work being done in the moment to meet the immediate need.

The outermost circle holds sufficient safety and sets the boundaries for the relational work; the inner gives purpose and the heft of achievement or change. But it

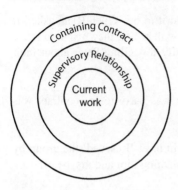

Figure 5.4   Concentric contracting.

is the middle circle where the real co-creative interchange happens. And it often happens through playfulness and discovery.

> To give a recent personal example, I was asked for a supervision session by a coach working in a complex situation and in a setting that I have no acquaintance with. As he described the circumstances around the supervision question, I became increasingly concerned at my apparent inability to grasp the detail and get a realistic picture of the problem.
>
> However, when I 'let go' and opened up my intuition, I saw (and offered) an intervention which had an immediate effect: this was the concentric contracting diagram. It was new to the coach, but it made instant sense without any need for complex explanations.
>
> We had found a useful space where my frame of reference and the supervisee's could meet. He was able to see that he had focused on the inner circle and neglected the middle one.

The supervision checklist

A useful tool for self-supervision for supervisors is the supervision checklist.[7] It is a way of making sure that the essentials are covered in any supervision session or piece.

- Has the contract for the work been fulfilled?
- Have you found the key issue, the out-of-awareness driving force that caused the problem?
- Has there been sufficient safety and protection for all involved?
- Does this piece of supervision enable the coach to grow?
- Is your working relationship OK-OK?

- And are you modelling a positive, authentic way forward?

The original checklist, created by Clarkson, has been developed by Marco Mazzetti as an operational model with the addition of an extra and important item:

- Establish a clear and appropriate contract.
- Identify key issues.
- Establish effective emotional contact with the supervisee.
- Make sure that the supervisee and the client are both adequately protected.
- Increase developmental directions.
- Increase awareness and effective use of parallel process.
- Develop an equal relationship.

These seven points may blend or overlap; for example, when the 'contracting is the work' key issues have been identified in the process, effective emotional contact may increase the awareness of parallel process; and co-working may involve increasing development and an equal, though asymmetric, relationship.

Doing supervision is not just the discussion of coaching but also a way of taking care of a colleague who has asked for supervision and, through them, their client. This may be the best way to ensure protection for both members of the coaching relationship.

The ability to attune to the coach's emotional experiences is a skill that every supervisor needs. Good emotional contact is the basis for good supervision; emotions are part of the supervision. We need to recognise them, name them and understand them, in order to develop effective awareness. Emotional issues experienced in supervision may also trigger insights, especially with experienced coaches who have greater self-awareness.

This is one way that supervision can be therapeutic. However, supervision may also reveal issues that need to be dealt with in therapy, for instance if a coach repeatedly brings the same issues and seems unable to make changes in spite of an apparent understanding, or if they are overly emotionally affected by their connection with some clients.

Bringing it together

A well-made contract results in a satisfying experience, full of empathy and rigour – but not rigid. It gives safety while supporting sometimes scary exploration.

The supervisor may have this checklist 'in their head' for the session (or for an entire piece of work) to make sure the contract was clear:

- Is the coach–client interaction OK-OK?
- Is the supervision relationship OK-OK?
- Does this work promote the development of the coach?
- Does it provide protection?

- Does it identify the issue that lies beneath any difficulties?
- Does it model a positive outcome and address any potential parallel process?

Most importantly, as they keep in mind the three functions of supervision, the supervisor will be alert to the psychological level of the contract:

- What is really going on here?
- Are all parties to the contract accounted for?
- Is the contract clear in all directions?

Any difficulty or lack of clarity in the process of making the supervision contract may be indicative of a problem with the coaching contract, with the client's work contract – or probably both.

The model of convergent process in Chapter 3 employs a triangle of contract, developmental direction and need for change (in the client's situation, in coaching, and in supervision). Through the lens of supervision, the coach and supervisor can explore these three facets of the coaching relationship and the work situation that generated the coaching contract.

The supervisor will be aware of their own process and reactions and able to use these as an instrument in supervision for 'outing' potential parallel process in any of the three. The use of the supervisor's self in providing information can make this a convergent process, highlighting the key issue that is causing the problem or 'stuck-ness'.

Contracting with yourself

A contract is a commitment to make a change or do something new. We may of course contract with – and for – ourselves to do something that is important to us. And, like all contracts, our personal contracts will work best if they are phrased positively and are realistic.

- What do you want to change or achieve as you read – and use – this book?
- How will you do that?
- How will you know you have reached your goal, and how will you celebrate?

Notes

1   Thanks to Geoff Watt for these observations.
2   Berne defined a contract as 'a mutual agreement towards a defined outcome' (1966). Muriel James in *Born to Win* says it is 'an Adult commitment to oneself and/or someone else to make a change'.
3   The questions for starting a new supervision alliance are based on a Solution Focus approach. The emphasis is on resource and potential. Thanks to BRIEF (previously the Brief Therapy Practice) for papers from which these questions are adapted.

4   The importance of understanding the three levels of the contract comes from the work of Eric Berne, writing about the multiple responsibilities of a therapist working in an organisation such as a hospital. He called the three levels 'administrative', 'professional' and 'psychological', and said that the latter would always determine the success or otherwise of the contract.

5   Fanita English published a short but very influential article in 1975, which has since become a key reference for transactional analysts.

6   Nelly Micholt in 1992 proposed variations of the equilateral triangle that show up the distortions in the contract.

7   The supervision checklist developed by Petruska Clarkson includes: contract fulfilled; key issue identified; reduction of probability of harm; increase professional development; modelling positive process; equal relationship (Clarkson 1992, p. 275–6). Marco Mazzetti (2007) elaborated this list and added 'establish emotional contact' as an essential aspect of effective supervision, stressing the importance of the emotional connection between supervisor and supervisee as a basis for transformational supervision. This Supervision Checklist has become a standard way of assessing effective supervision (and is used as such in TA supervision exams, and, adapted by us for assessment on our training courses).

Chapter 6

Success and safety
The context and ethics of supervision

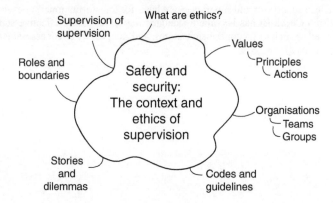

In a book about supervision for coaches, why are we devoting a whole chapter to ethics?

'Ethics' is often assumed to deal only with questions of right and wrong, but in practice this proves not to be so – ethics is far more complex and interesting than that. In fact, the values that underpin and inform all we do, that hold us to account, are the reason we want to do this work. As a colleague writes:

> Because I don't feel judged, or that I need to prove;
> Because I can be in relationship, yet separate;
> And because I can be intrigued by the other;
> And am accepted for who I am.[1]

Why are we concerned to challenge – to bother grappling with concerns of principle, to live with our own inadequacies and frustrations, to confront fear and shame – and to find courage and compassion for ourselves and for others?

In the previous chapter, where we explored contracts, the aim was clarity of purpose and process; to bring everything into the light. Ethics, on the other hand, deals with the persistent complexity and messiness of human relations in all their ambiguity and uncertainty. Because of this, ethical discussions are sometimes perceived as a struggle; however, it is good to remember that our aim should not be to bring everyone to the same point of view, but to build awareness and keep the dialogue going.

In this chapter, we will define 'the ethical territory', identifying some of its potential minefields and suggesting ways of relating beliefs, principles and practices to the question: 'How do we know we are being ethical here?'

We will also cover some legal aspects of supervision, its 'mores' (the cultural basis for our ethical assumptions), and link these with insights from egostate and script theory. We will ask how our ability to notice ethical boundaries may be compromised by operating in an increasingly 'me-centred', 'self-entitled', isolated and fearful world: how this impacts on our supervisees' work with their coaching clients – and how all these considerations may show up in supervision.

Exploring the territory

In the supervision relationship, the territory of ethical debate is often the place where permission needs to be given, both 'down the line' (supervisor to supervisee to client) and also 'up the line', with supervisor and supervisee both learning to recognise when the client has made an informed choice that is valid in their circumstances.

One of the jobs that may need to be done in supervision is to help a coach to 're-story' a particular piece of work, an event or client relationship – to begin to see it differently. They may feel that the work went badly, or be embarrassed about their own thinking and behaviour. At the heart of this may well be a dawning awareness that something was not quite ethical. Our job is to help the coach see the situation clearly, take the learning and commit to any actions that are necessary to rectify it. But in doing this, how do we make sure we are not rescuing or colluding?

We want to challenge you to think about 'ethics' with us, and to go on thinking about it, because ethics are those pesky little things that creep in and crop up all over the place in the work of a coach – and therefore in the work of the supervisor. Along with contracting, ethical debate is at the heart of supervision and provides a lot of the testing, challenging, chewy (and yes, fun) discussion that takes place in this relationship!

What we mean by ethics

Conversations about whether something is ethical or not often reveal profound differences in expectations and assumptions, and can force those involved to confront their own prejudices and fears, their timidity in action or narrowness in thinking. It's important that coach and supervisor start with some shared basic ethical beliefs and guidelines; in working together, these will increasingly be explored and tested.

Table 6.1 Personal ethics; an example

Core Beliefs	what we believe; what is most important to us	people are equal and intrinsically valuable everyone can grow and change we can all contribute to our world community personal integrity
Ethical Principles	guidelines we derive from our personal values	treat everyone with respect honour commitments take appropriate responsibility be transparent in communication build relationships on trust and openness;
Practical actions and behaviours	what we do as a result	give clear explanations to all about roles and interventions contract with all parties maintain good boundaries listen carefully give feedback respectfully keep to agreed timings

So what is ethics? Fundamentally it is the container for establishing, at the level of behaviour and intention, what is – or is not – OK in a situation. Sometimes, what we describe as our 'ethic' comes from our religious or cultural context. It may then be so completely taken for granted that we don't know it's there till it is violated or challenged in some way. We all have some core beliefs that we have acquired, whether deliberately or by osmosis, throughout our lives so far; some of these will be 'deep' beliefs and values, so much a part of us that we are not even aware they can be questioned; others will be more conscious, because we have arrived at them as a result of reflecting on our personal experience. In the context of coaching and supervision, our ethical beliefs may also be strongly influenced by the training we've had and the world we've worked in.

It is from all of these that we form our personal ethic. What we actually do in our professional practice and our personal interactions and relationships will grow from these principles, and Table 6.1 gives some examples of these connections.

Beliefs and values

In Chapter 2, we explored ideas from TA that enable us to understand more about how we think and communicate. Using them helps us open up what we mean when we talk about ethics – and deal with some of the confusions we may encounter. We can look into this further by considering the difference between morality and ethics.

As society has changed over millennia, human beings have changed little physiologically. But cultural evolution – including religion, social organisation, art and science – has taken over as a marker of stages in society, and at each stage core values are expressed in different ways and with different emphases.

Values are certainly an indicator of change and a key feature of the Cultural Parent. Socio-economic development influences – in fact transforms – people's basic values and beliefs, and does so in a roughly predictable fashion.

Morality is a constant we can look to for a sense of consistency and continuity – it is part of the social or cultural Parent shared by members of a group or society; it forms part of the individual's Parent egostate. Our frame of reference will include both a moral viewpoint that we have acquired in our family and culture, and our individual response to it of acceptance or rejection.

Ethics is very different. It is a parental function of the integrating Adult, aware of the context, the situation, the contributing factors and the needs of the participants. It always is – and needs to be – relativistic: we change our ethical response as the situation changes.[2]

Sometimes, people find it hard to move from the clear, pre-existing moral stance to the situational, growing, vibrant world of ethical decisions; it seems so much easier to look to a constant Parent to tell us what is right or wrong.

Arriving at a personal ethical place is like an ongoing conversation between Parent and Adult, sorting out the relevant issues and shifting the frame of reference as we learn more about ourselves and the world we live in. Part of this will be our cultural script – the part of our 'frame' that may either limit or support us in our decision-making.

But our cultural script can be changed as well. That ongoing conversation enables societies to update the cultural Parent and (hopefully) integrate beneficent values, while holding a consistent morality that gives meaning to the culture: to protect but not limit the social Child and to develop a responsible and empathic Adult. This is what we mean by social change (Figure 6.1).[3]

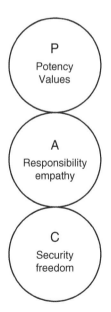

Figure 6.1 Integrated egostates.

Source: Adapted from Drego 2006.

Some situations can cause us to take a fresh look at our values:

> Maria began to feel uncertain about her work overall, rather than about any particular piece of coaching. Talking about this feeling, she realised that she no longer kept a balance in her portfolio between well-paid organisational work and work for voluntary associations, community projects or other groups that she cared about.
>
> Her everyday activities had ceased to be in tune with her core values.

Or, we might find that the principles we have adhered to for years can be adjusted:

> Pablo was determined that he would not work in corporates – a principle which he believed derived from his conviction that it was important to only use his skills to support those in the helping professions and for the development of people in public service. But he gradually began to recognise that people are people – doing the best they can for themselves, their colleagues and their families, whatever environment they choose to work in – and that he was judging workers in corporate environment as being somehow less worthy as human beings!
>
> Why shouldn't he use his empathic capacities and skills with them and make a difference to those in business organisations too? His personal values didn't change but he was able to expand his guidelines about where he could contribute to a healthier society.

Both these stories show coaches reflecting on their values for themselves. Another story tells how this may happen between members in a group:

> Isla trained to be a supervisor in a group of coaches, all of whom had academic qualifications in coaching and some of whom also worked in academic environments, teaching and training others and contributing to research on coaching and coach supervision. They all aspired to deliver large corporate contracts at high fee-rates, and talked a lot about their qualifications and their work.
>
> Isla had come to coaching and supervision via a very different route. She didn't have a degree, but had trained as a coach with an internationally accredited school whose training was substantive, practical, and hands on. She was now a trainer with that same organisation and had many hours of experience under her belt. Her passion was to use her skills in supporting communities which were often neglected or marginalised, and to help people within them to get a chance of a better life. Consequently, her coaching work was typically in projects which were low profile and paid low fee rates.
>
> Isla always felt somewhat daunted in the company of her training group and, truth to tell, they did patronise her – just a bit. This left her feeling isolated and unsure of herself in their company. Her inability to truly value her own capability, experience and work was starting to get in the way of her

contributing to her own and her colleagues' learning.

The dynamic in the group was becoming increasingly unconducive to mutual support and learning, until the day when Isla was asked to talk about the current contexts in which she was coaching and supervising: the rest of the group were stunned to discover what challenging environments she was working in. They recognised how much courage she had to find in order to engage with these difficult situations, and the very high level of skill needed to create and maintain a secure environment with trusting relationships so her clients could do the work they needed to do. The group were honest and generous in their responses and, as she saw herself reflected in their eyes – the eyes of this group in which she had always felt so small – she recognised that she was the equal of anyone in it. And so did they.

The discussion which followed illuminated for them all the assumptions and value-judgements that they had been making about each other, based simply on the different environments in which they had chosen to work. And, of course, they began to question themselves about the extent to which their biases, blind spots and prejudices might be leaking into their work as supervisors.

There are some core values that almost all humans care deeply about – fairness, justice, love, respect, loyalty, prevention of harm and respect for the sacred. If we look for commonly-agreed values on which to base a set of ethical principles, such as might become a code of conduct or practice, we find:

- Equality – everyone is equal, in any society and throughout the world, and is equally treated in law.
- Dignity – each person is intrinsically valuable (as described in the Universal Declaration of Human Rights, 1948).
- Self-determination – everyone is free to decide on their own future, within the limits of national laws and taking into account the needs of themselves and others. Everyone can learn from experience and take responsibility for themselves without damaging the world or the freedom of others.
- Health – every individual has the right to physical and mental stability, and this right should be actively protected.
- Safety – everyone should be able to develop in a safe environment.
- Reciprocity or interdependence – every person lives in a world with other people, and is thus mutually involved in the welfare of others. They are mutually dependent on others in the development of reciprocal security.[4]

These principles have been much discussed in many contexts. In medical ethics, for instance, they are summarised as the principles of: autonomy, beneficence, non-maleficence ('do no harm') and respect for human dignity. In discussions in groups, values that often come up are: dignity, integrity, security, mutuality, self-determination; principles often include: empowerment, commitment, beneficence, 'do no harm', confidentiality, honesty, transparency.

An individual may also hold a set of beliefs around what is or isn't ethical in their personal life which is different from the beliefs that inform their professional life. So their ethics are boundaried by their environment.

> If this is not true for both coach and supervisor, what challenges might that create in the relationship?

Principles and guidelines for action

This is a key challenge for the supervisor: 'Is it wrong, or is it just something I wouldn't do?'

How do different people decide the principles that guide their work?

If you're working with a number of coaches (new coaches, experienced coaches, coaches from differing backgrounds and trainings), you will constantly be surprised, delighted and amazed at the things they and their clients get up to and the pickles they get themselves into – and out of!

As their supervisor, you will need to be able to work with a coach in a very discerning way, one that helps to discriminate between what is truly OK or not OK – right or wrong – and what simply represents a proper difference between how the two of you might view or approach a particular situation.

One of the delights of ethical questions is that there is so rarely only one answer, and often many choices for a resolution. This can be one of the richest areas for mutual sharing and learning.

Our ethics are often embodied in our principles – the way we bring our core values, philosophy and beliefs into our actions. In our professional practice with clients, other professionals, colleagues and the community, these provide guidelines for behaviour:

- Respect – for every person, whatever characteristics or qualities they may have.
- Empowerment – encouraging everyone to take responsibility for their own destiny and to develop themselves.
- Protection – caring both physically and mentally for oneself and others, on the basis of the uniqueness and value of every living being.
- Responsibility – being aware of the consequences of one's actions as a coach, supervisor or colleague.
- Involvement – a genuine interest in the well-being of the other.[5]

How do we move from values and guidelines to what we do in the moment?

We may find a formula that appeals to us – such as the one Roger Steare proposes in his book, 'Ethicability', where he asks how we ' decide what's "RIGHT" and find the courage to do it'[6]:

- R: what are the rules?
- I: are we acting with integrity?

- G: who is this good for?
- H: who might we harm?
- T: what's the truth?

He encourages people to think through dilemmas with the aid of a straightforward schema of preparation, decision and testing, based on insights from moral philosophy and human psychology:

- Preparation: how do we feel? Who's involved? What are the facts? What sort of dilemma is this? What are our intentions? What are our options? Have we thought creatively?
- Decide what's 'right', using the questions above.
- Test our decision: how would we feel in the other person's shoes? What would be fair and reasonable? What would be the adult thing to do? What would build trust and respect? What would stand the test of time? Have we the courage to do what's right? And, what can we learn from this dilemma?

Or, we could take a more reflective approach to arrive at a place where we can apply these ideas and be sure of our position.

Michael Carroll proposes that we can acquire 'ethical maturity'.[7] Just as we grow up physically, we develop our ethical thinking from childhood through adolescence to adulthood, making decisions in different ways at different stages. We can see this as moving from a fixed Parent ethic to an integrating Adult response, taking account of all the factors rather than thinking that we just 'know'.

Ethical maturity is:

- having the reflective, rational, intuitive and emotional capacity to decide actions are either right or wrong;
- having the courage and resilience to implement our decisions;
- being accountable for ethical decisions made publicly or privately;
- sensitivity, thoughtfulness, discernment, accountability and the ability to implement our decisions, to live with them and to learn from the experience.

And these are all part of developing a state of ethical maturity.

Ethics in practice

So, what do we actually do? Accrediting bodies such as the International Coach Federation or European Mentoring and Coaching Council require that we conduct ourselves in accordance with their codes of ethics in all interactions, including coach training, coach mentoring and coach supervisory activities. More information about these can be found at the end of this book.

Whichever association and code we have chosen, the best way to get thinking about how to apply an ethical code is to wrestle with some challenging situations. To prompt you in doing this – individually or with others such as a peer group – at the end of the chapter we have included several stories that have been brought to supervision and provided challenges for everyone involved.

But, before we move on, let's see what we can learn from previous chapters and consider in more detail the distinct functions of supervision (management, support, development) in terms of ethics.

In the balance of functions diagram (Figure 3.2) the 'management' or accounting corner is where ethical procedures are most apparent. The place of this function is precisely to maintain an ethical standard in practice: the supervisee learns by considering, first their supervisor's and then their own, attention to what is and is not OK in their work.

It is in breaches in this area that ethics codes may kick in: how well are boundaries kept? Is the coach competent and upholding standards? And perhaps most importantly, is the work within the contract – or is the contract distorted and in need of renegotiation?

Following this obvious ethical area, we turn to 'support': this function, essential as it is in resourcing the supervisee, carries the risk of the supervisor falling into reassurance: many new coaches, and many experienced practitioners as well, go to supervision with a desire for comfort. This is fertile ground for a rupture in the supervisory relationship; the temptation is to sooth and to be a 'good parent'. In supervision, even experienced coaches ask for reassurance that they have 'done the right thing'.

> Kirk and his supervisor had a good working relationship that had been developed over several years. Kirk both changed his professional context and re-developed his own sense of his professional identity quite frequently. In spite of being highly skilled and widely experienced he often came to supervision seemingly wanting to hear that his latest venture was 'OK' with his supervisor. She (his supervisor) felt that this was an ongoing feature of their sessions, and also that it was necessary – she sensed a fragility in Kirk that needed nurture. And she sometimes ended the sessions feeling that she had not done a good job. After thinking this through she chose a time when Kirk was reporting on a successful project and, after giving appropriate strokes, moved into a more challenging approach in the next item on his list. His response was instant and surprising 'It's so good when we do real supervision!'

Teasing this out should lead to the third corner, 'development': this is the cutting edge, the real challenge of truly co-creative work, where ethics becomes a more subtle process of attention to the psychological contract and to 'what is really going on'.

Where and how will we encounter ethical issues?

We may be supervising a coach who is carrying something that belongs to the wider system, or working within an organisation ourselves, or encountering issues in one-to-one work which concern the actual supervisory relationship.

Teams and groups – supervision in organisations

As we aim to work ethically in organisations, we can sometimes come up against a culture that seems fixed or rule-bound. This may be due to anxiety about an uncertain future, changes happening or proposed, or a sense of risk around doing anything different to the perceived norm.

As we move from 'knowing' to learning, enabling a reflective approach, we can work towards tolerating complexity and risk. We can then support people in being proactive rather than reactive – looking for long-term development rather than short-term expediency, sharing in planning and decision-making.[8]

In-house coaches (or groups of external coaches working for a single organisation) are regularly encouraged to attend supervision in groups so that the organisation employing them can benefit from their shared experience and learning. Sometimes there will also be an economic argument for group supervision. In this situation, issues of confidentiality may need even more careful handling – for the clients will often be easily identifiable by other members of the group.

All of the things that are true about supervision groups (described in Chapter 7) are also true here. In addition, in-house coaches may not be signed up to a professional body, so they will need to decide what their ethical code is – the organisation itself may have the basis of one that can be built on. They will also need to know what their contract with the organisation is: what are allowable topics, and what aren't. Some organisations really only want their coaches to work on career development, whilst for others 'anything goes' – and there can be almost anything in between.

Coaches also need to know what their boundaries are in other ways. For instance, they may be asked to support people exiting through a redundancy programme – but themselves be so angry with the organisation (or experiencing 'survivor guilt' because they are staying) that they can't do the work authentically. It's worth surfacing a lot of this stuff early on with the group – and probably with the sponsor with whom you initially discuss setting up a supervision group.

A typical supervision session will be very similar to any other group, with the proviso that time may need to be made for updating the supervisor, and other group members, on any particular organisational changes that could impact on the coaches or their clients and form a backdrop to the work.

Roles and boundaries

Supervision may be a therapeutic encounter, but it is not therapy. This is also true of coaching. Close attention to this boundary is an ethical responsibility of the supervisor.

A number of different (and potentially overlapping) professional and non-professional roles share similar competencies, for example, coaching, mentoring, counselling, therapy, consulting and befriending. The client may sometimes be unclear about the differences or want one person to perform several different roles for them. At some level, as long as the contracting and re-contracting is clear, anything is possible; however, it is legitimate for a supervisor to check with their supervisee that this actually is coaching.

Boundaries, both of activity and information, need constant review. This is very often at the heart of ethical dilemmas, particularity when working in extended organisational systems.

Two short stories illustrate how boundaries can become blurred:

> An internal coach reported in supervision that every session with one client very soon became a long ramble about the client's domestic problems, and how anxiety about these prevented him from doing anything to meet the outcomes that had been agreed. The coach, who was not very long qualified, felt stuck with no further options. She was relieved when her supervisor suggested that the client's problems might be more appropriately addressed through counselling (his organisation had provision for that). The coach had felt responsible for accepting anything the client brought, and at that stage didn't have the experience to identify a needed boundary. Learning when to refer on, and being clear about what is included in coaching and what isn't, is key for new coaches.
>
> Another much more experienced coach had a client who was leaving his organisation – with their blessing. They had provided coaching to help him get clear about how he wanted to exit, and what he was going to do with his career going forward. The first few sessions were extremely productive and an exit plan was designed and agreed. The future was becoming increasingly clear – and there were still more sessions to come. In fact, coach and client were so aligned in terms of ideas for setting up a new business that it looked like an ideal opportunity for them both to work together. They were a great match in terms of their professional background and skills; they felt they worked together incredibly well. The coach excitedly told his supervisor all about this – and was quite shocked when his supervisor questioned this merging of coach-client and colleague-colleague relationships.

Withholding

There are potentially unhelpful consequences to coaches being trained in the non-directive model, and of course this may affect supervisors as well.

The coach may report they are being scrupulous in not putting their opinions into the coaching space because, quite rightly if it's a coaching contract, they don't want to be mentoring, consulting, teaching, or doing anything that isn't coaching.

However, the client experience of this can be that the coach has information the client doesn't have, or maybe doesn't know they don't have ('I don't know what I don't know').

The client may well think that the coach is deliberately withholding; they may therefore feel – when they don't get the answer right or flounder around unable to identify where to seek the next insight or how to design the next action – that they are in some way being set up to fail. The client may then either actively challenge the coach, or passively withdraw from the coaching relationship. Either way, this issue will turn up in supervision.

Whilst it's essential for coaches to give their clients as much opportunity as possible to work out their own methods and discover what's important for themselves, if the coach knows that there's some information, actual data in the form of available help systems, training courses or support facilities, and the client doesn't – why wouldn't the coach tell the client?

This withholding of data has the potential to establish an inequality of power in the coach/client relationship. If the coach is withholding data from the client that they might find valuable, but either can't or haven't found a way to uncover no matter how hard they've tried, then it puts the coach in a position of inappropriate power.

That feels really uncomfortable and wrong: fear of being parental or of inappropriately taking an authority role is reasonable; but it isn't Parental to share what you know: it is an Adult role. We are offering the client a chance to expand their information base, on the understanding that they are perfectly capable of rejecting the offer if it's not what they want or need.

Another version of withholding is even more insidious – and can happen all too easily if the supervisor is thinking or feeling something which they are not willing to share with the coach. The supervisor puts themselves in danger of moving into that controlling place of, 'I know something that you don't know and I'm going to decide when you're ready to hear it'.

The starting point for resolving this is that the supervisor needs to model equality of power in the relationship; because it is a more productive learning space, giving the coach confidence and permission to work in this way with their own clients.

Holding to the purity of a 'non-directive' approach may actually mask something else – most often that either the supervisor or the coach-supervisee is nervous of being direct in their communication and uncertain of their ability to offer an observation without attachment. Sometimes, the supervisor may realise they don't believe the supervisee is sufficiently robust to hear what is being offered. At this point, the supervisor may need to ask themselves if they are 'Rescuing' the coach, and whether they have got into a parallel process that could have further implications. Once recognised by supervisor and supervisee (and subsequently coach and client), change can happen and progress can be made.

This takes us back to the contract: how we can contract in a way that enables all parties to declare the boundaries of what will be asked for, what will be offered, and under what circumstances?

Minding the gap

As well as the 'big-picture' ethical areas we need to take account of in supervision and coaching, there are moment-by-moment micro-issues that affect the more supportive or challenging relationships.

This is where we encounter what Sue Eusden describes as the necessity of risk[9]:

> The challenge for supervisees is in bringing the work for scrutiny, and this involves bringing themselves as well as their client. If they are over-invested in looking good, or with the fault staying in the client, then this can undermine the heart of the relationship and the work.
>
> Risk and uncertainty are inescapable existential challenges that face all coaches and clients (and even all human beings!). Often, talk is of minimizing risks by skilful assessment.
>
> We need skilful assessment to maximize risks! Risk-taking is an enlivening process in which we may engage with difference, conflict and play as the focus in the work. (Eusden 2011, p. 110)

No matter what safeguards we put in place, sometimes we will have a sense that we have (possibly potentially) acted unethically. Not through deliberate action, but more through inattention: going for an easy option such as reassurance rather than questioning the coach/supervisee, or simply making poor interventions. Whether we are working in a two-person or two-person-plus way, there will be times when we fail to tune in to the other and put the relationship at risk. In other words, we make mistakes, and these are a part of learning – and being human!

Eusden goes on to talk of 'Minding the Gap', paying attention to the conscious/unconscious space between supervisor and supervisee – the space between our own intention and its impact on the other. It is in this gap that an intervention intended to be transformative can be experienced as critical, over-intrusive or even unethical.

Attending to our interventions and their impact – staying curious about what emerges, and so becomes available to explore any dynamic disturbance – can feel risky, even scary, as deeper, more unconscious forms of relating emerge. This 'working edge' may be in the ruptures rather than the empathic enquiries. This is where the quality of attention really matters.

Supervision is where we enact, through parallel process, whatever is going wrong in the work. It is in itself a place where minding the gap is paramount, not just a place where we can reflect on the gap 'in the practice'. This is the essence of properly functioning supervision: its effect is that growth and healing happen for coach, client – and supervisor as well.

Getting support – supervision for your supervision

Every supervisor needs their own support, whether through a peer group or individual supervision. While there are many specific items that might be brought to supervision – some of them exampled in the stories we are using in each chapter as illustrations – here, we have chosen to look at some more general areas that may intrude from time to time.

Sometimes, as a supervisor, you can feel that you are holding the whole of that 8-eyed model, all the people in it, their wider system and the profession, and your own work, all on your own shoulders. You need to have somewhere to take that – and it's called 'supervision for your supervision'.

There are a number of ways to do this. Some supervisors choose peer supervision, one-to-one or in a group, sharing the job with other supervisors. Some hire an 'external' supervisor for an individual relationship or to run a supervisors' supervision group. Either way works, and the same rules of engagement apply: good contracting, making sure that you are addressing all aspects of the triangle equally over time, looking for parallel process, and so on. In addition, it is useful to be clear whether you are getting supervision on your supervision – or do you also want to bring your own coaching work?

Many coaches who train as supervisors say that it makes them better coaches (which is great), but it is important to remember that, whilst the two roles contain many shared competencies, they are different – and that difference matters, especially to the client.

- What is the most desirable and practical way for you to get supervision on your supervision? It may be that a particular supervisor or group attracts you; it may simply be what you can easily access, find time for, or afford.
- Do you notice any resistance to doing this?
- If you are both a coach and a supervisor of coaches, how do you distinguish between the two roles?
- What is your identity in each role – is it overlapping, and if so where, and is that OK or not?
- How do you want to get supervision for each?
- Are you looking for similarity or differences between them – in the way that you are and the way that you work?
- What can each role learn from the other?

Stories and histories

As we saw in Chapter 4, 'stories' are how we create and re-create our world and influence the worlds of others. In supervision, both parties need to be alert to the stories they are telling and hearing, and particularly notice the beliefs, both enabling and disabling, that seem to be embedded in them.

The interior story being told – but not necessarily voiced – also needs to be listened to 'with the ear of the heart' (St Benedict's Rule). This will often reveal the deeper inhibitors for supervisor, coach and client – and the yearnings that may not be truly expressed.

An example might be the client not feeling they're 'good enough': the coach/ supervisee and the supervisor feel the same – and all of this will be expressed in the most subtle of discounts.

- What limiting beliefs have you noticed that might inhibit your ability to be truly open to your supervisee's story?
- What are your own strongest enabling beliefs?
- Who would you work with as a supervisee, and who would you not – and why?

In both individual and group contexts for supervision, the supervisor needs to be willing to be open and vulnerable to their own experience as well as to the supervisee's. It is therefore important for the supervisor to understand how they may feel differently in these two contexts – what comes up for them, what their experience of intimacy in one-to-one relationships has been and also what their history is in group settings.

For many supervisors it is easier (whether or not it is desirable) to maintain a distance from the emotion of a group than it is from that of one other person. In both contexts, the supervisee(s) will also be bringing their own history, and may have an unconscious preference for playing out their script either in a one-to-one setting or in a group.

What is your experience of working – one-to-one or in groups – as a coach or as a supervisor?

- What comes up for you?
- What is easy and OK, what seems more difficult?
- How might this influence your supervisee(s)?
- What do you need to develop in yourself?

Practicalities – things we need to know

Professional ethics are enshrined in codes of conduct. It's important to know which professional body your coach supervisee has signed up to. Coaches should be holding themselves accountable to something outside themselves, essentially by having membership of some professional organisation. Take a good look at their ethical code, and think about whether you can support this coach in working within it.

We need to consider the business of actually doing the work from two points of view. One is what we need to do in order to be working ethically, such as keeping notes and getting our own supervision. The other is just as important: paying attention to the moment-by-moment transactions and being aware when our relationship with a supervisee is at risk of disruption. Paying attention is the most essential and significant part of supervision, the most generous gift we offer our supervisees – and the most effective.

Constraints on supervisors to disclose

First, the 'Have-to's: there is, of course, The Law! It is important to know what behaviour by the coach might be in violation of the prevailing system. Our working practice has to demonstrate the principles we operate from and that they are within the general culture.

Legal contexts differ from one country to another, so it is important to be familiar, at least in outline, with those of any country you work in – or where your coach-supervisee works. Once you know the general principles, you can be clear with coaches what you would need to disclose if you had information. This clarity should be part of the overall contract at the start of a supervisory partnership.

In the UK, for instance, there is an obligation to pass on to appropriate authorities any awareness of child-abuse, money-laundering, terrorist activity or conspiracy to commit such an activity. In addition, you need to be aware of data protection regulations (basically: not to pass on any information without permission and to only keep data that clients have agreed to you holding).

If you think that someone may be a danger to themselves or others, you must be clear with them that, unless they take some action to change the situation and get help – see their doctor, tell the boss, etc., then you must do so.

These responsibilities apply both to you as supervisor and to the coaches you work with – they also need to be aware of their necessary responses to clients if any of the above become apparent in coaching.

Keeping notes and records

For the initial contracting, both supervisor and coach may want to capture the agreement between them in some detail, and they will also want to record any significant changes in the contract as they arise over time. However, once the contract has been established, though the coach-supervisee needs to keep whatever helps them to maintain their optimum learning state, note-keeping by the supervisor should be kept to a minimum.

For the supervisor, we suggest that only the main agenda items for the session, the commitments made on either side or items to be carried forward, are recorded on a session-by-session basis. If additional particular themes or issues do need to be captured, the language used should always be the supervisee's actual language.

To give full attention to all of the information available – visual, auditory, kinaesthetic and intuitive – both parties need to be fully present to themselves, to each other and to the relationship: we are strongly against the growing practice of either party entering the session onto a computer in real-time!

> Helena worked with a client as his coach over a two-year period. He was the MD of his company and it was a difficult time, with many restructurings. He had an extremely challenging boss – the owner of the company. Many of his coaching sessions were about how he was going to manage this relationship in a way that allowed both him and the organisation to be successful.

He was very overweight and unfit, and sometimes exhibited signs of stress such as shouting at people in the office. For a number of months he had been prescribed anti-depressants by his doctor, something he told Helena about, but had not disclosed at work.

The coaching work concluded when things seemed to be going well for him and the wider organisation. About six months later, he emailed Helena to say that he was in dispute with the organisation. He had now left, but each party was suing the other.

He and, independently, the HR director of his company, asked Helena to report on the work she had done with him and give her view as to his mental and physical health.

After some discussion, the HR director accepted that Helena should not – and would not – break any confidentiality boundaries.

But, in the event, the client gave her his permission to disclose everything.

Look at this dilemma through the lens of your own beliefs and principles.

- If you had been the coach, what would you have done?
- If you were the coach's supervisor, how would you have worked with them on this?

How do we manage complexity?

The following stories and dilemmas will, we hope, prompt you to think through your own ethical stance. When shared with other colleagues, they may lead to useful discussion and even, maybe, some re-thinking.

Making assessments

A number of coaches were invited to coach a population of managers – against a set of pre-agreed leadership behaviours which the organisation wished them to demonstrate consistently.

The coaching work was to be done in a mix of small groups and one-to-ones. The coaches were asked to keep records of the work of the clients in the sessions, and at the end report on the extent to which they believed each of them would now be able and willing to demonstrate those behaviours back in the business.

- If you heard this from a supervisee who was one of the group of coaches, what would your reaction be? Your response will depend on what you believe about coaching, about roles in organisations, and what is most important to you in your own work.

And the story continues:

Several coaches turned the job down. One who accepted it only really understood towards the end of the work what was being asked of her. Once she realised, she wrote the reports together with her clients, thus getting their agreement – but without the knowledge of the organisation.

This solution might raise further questions, so how can we find our way through them?

Gender and sexuality

Supervision for coaches is a very new field and there are still questions to be asked – and understandings to emerge – about what the psychological contract actually is in this relationship: what should a healthy contract include; what is the psychological nature of a supervision/coaching relationship?

If we were talking about counselling or therapy, we'd need to include sexuality and gender, and yet this is rarely raised as something to be paid attention to in the coach/client or the supervisor/supervisee contract. But surely this psychological level exists, as it does in any other relationship?

So, what do we want to do about gender and sexuality as part of our contract? If we decide to include it, how? If we choose to deny it, what might be the consequences?

For instance, coaches often talk about 'chemistry meetings'. How OK is it to describe meetings in this way? There is certainly more to 'chemistry' between people than sex, but the implication is that it's somehow below the radar and that, whilst we don't really know it, there is an attraction which is not specifically named and understood – and 'attraction' in our culture can come with quite a lot of baggage. Often the invitation is into an unhelpful egostate: for instance, overly-nurturing Parent. This may disable us from effectively fulfilling our professional role.

- How do you think about sexuality and gender in the coach/client or supervision relationship?
- Think about any experiences you yourself have had, either as a coach or a supervisor – how did you feel?
- And what did you do?

This story of inappropriate texting is an example:

A newly-hired senior client account manager chose Lucy after interviewing two other (male) coaches and then specifically asking HR to present a female coach to him. Their first two coaching sessions focussed on his new role. They were professional and productive. After the second session she received a text from him: 'Do you have any tattoos – I couldn't see one?'

Lucy texted back, 'FYI I've just received a text from you which clearly was meant for someone else.'

She immediately received a return text – 'Oh no – it's for you – Do you?'

Lucy didn't reply. Before the next meeting he emailed saying, 'You didn't answer my question'.

She ignored it. They had their third session and nothing was said about this by either of them. After that, Lucy received another email – 'I forgot to ask about your tattoos!'

She took this to her supervision group.

- If you had been a member of the supervision group, what would you have said in the discussion?

Sharing dilemmas

This is a useful exercise to do in a peer-group of supervisors.

One person relates a recent situation where he or she was uncertain what to do, because of conflicting factors or ethical questions.

Everyone states their initial response.

Then, all take time to think how that tracks back to the personal values and principles we identified earlier.

In the subsequent discussion each person explains their thinking – or their new insights.

It may be that people have different views; the value of the exercise is in the discussion and the increasing awareness for each person of their own beliefs and how they want to act.

And finally, a nicely complicated situation which came out of the blue:

Laundering dirty information

Ruth introduced Emily to a potential coachee in one of her client organisations.

Emily had worked for Ruth in another organisation, so knew who Ruth was coaching there.

Emily told the potential coachee that Ruth was a great coach; that she was working with some very senior, well-known people in the same industry; and by chance, one of those people was the client's industry hero – the person he aspired to be!

Great intro for Ruth.

Ruth met the client for an exploratory conversation and they got on well, but she was concerned that they were too alike; both very high-energy. Ruth requested that the client consider another coach, her colleague Malek, who might be more helpful in supporting him to meet his coaching goals – which included understanding and working with people who were different from him.

The client met Malek, who also thought he'd be a better coach for the client than Ruth; but the client still wanted Ruth: 'very easy to be with' – and his hero's coach to boot!

Ruth brought this dilemma to her supervision group (which included Malek) as she wanted to 'find a way of not getting here again' – i.e. the client choosing her when she felt she wasn't the best choice for them. She also said that, by the time she came to take her turn as supervisee, she was feeling oddly queasy as she thought about the whole situation.

As she unpacked the story in supervision, Ruth noticed that both she and the client had been somewhat, albeit unintentionally, 'set-up' by Emily. The new client had not been offered a clean space in which to meet Ruth, and she hadn't realised there was a bigger story he was sitting with: about her as a coach.

There was also a light-bulb moment in the supervision, when Ruth realised that Emily had broken Ruth's confidentiality and, even more importantly, her clients'. Emily had not been given permission to talk to anyone at all about who was working with Ruth as their coach, or even which organisations she was working in.

What had Emily been thinking!

Ruth was mortified – it had never occurred to her to have such an overt discussion with Emily. She'd assumed that 'everyone – especially people I like and respect – holds boundaries the way I do'.

Ruth committed to talk to Emily about this violation of confidentiality and get a better contract with her as a colleague about how they worked, together and in each other's client organisations. She also planned to tell her clients what had happened and apologise to them.

In the meantime, Ruth also realised that she could, and would, do a good job for her new client – but there was a possibility of him working with Malek in a later phase of his development.

She also realised that she'd had another demonstration of the fact that when she had a feeling, she should bring something to supervision – and she was right!

When the discussion was opened to the group, Malek spoke up:

> Emily was one of his supervisees! Was she going to talk to him about this when she next came to supervision? Emily knows he knows Ruth, but it isn't clear if she knows they are in the same supervision group!

Ruth hadn't remembered that Malek was Emily's supervisor. Malek was left with knowing something he couldn't share with his supervisee, as he'd learnt it in the confidential space of his supervision group.

In Malek's own words: how was he going to launder this 'dirty information'?

Notes

1   Thanks to Sheena Reed.
2   This perspective comes from Carlo Moiso, in a round table discussion in 2006 (Cornell 2006), where he distinguishes morality and ethics. Morality, he says, for instance in perception of right and wrong, is part of the social Parent – it is 'constant, and by this constancy morality gives us a sense of consistency'; ethics, on the other hand, 'is the parental function of the integrating Adult because it changes constantly' and therefore recognises, and works with, the knowledge that what is right for one client is not right for another. So, in this brief extract, we have the essential and different notions of the indispensible solidity of the social Parent, and the continual responsiveness of the integrating Adult of the individual person/practitioner.
3   In a new development of the egostate model, Pearl Drego extends the theory to draw attention to the altruistic qualities of people and their beneficent intentions in working with others. She suggests that up-dating and integrating take place within *each* egostate and *between* the three egostates and that this process engages the total personality in enabling helpfulness, responsibility, compassion, service and so on to flow (2006, 2009). In the 'updated and integrated' PAC model, we find (and experience) Parent potency, Adult responsibility and a Child with the security of inner freedom. 'Furthermore, as the intra-psychic attraction between egostates deepens, so does interpersonal connectivity with others' (2006:99).
4   These value descriptions are based on those of the European Association for Transactional Analysis (EATA), (EATA 2008). EATA, as a federation of national TA associations within Europe, has created a framework for understanding an ethical approach. This includes some basic assumptions which we think are valuable to note: *There is a close connection between ethics and practice*: behaviour can be ethical or not, depending on whether or not it promotes the well-being of self and others. *Ethics is a general framework, which guides a practitioner in providing a professional service and always underpins practice.* It is not limited to solving difficult and problematic situations. *Ethics identifies values that help people to realise their potential as human beings; values underpin ethical principles as guidelines to actualise values. Principles, which underpin deontological norms, are a guideline to professional practice.* Links to the EATA website can be found in the notes on Ethical Codes at the end of this book.
5   These principles also are based on those suggested by EATA (2008).
6   Roger Steare, in his book *Ethicability*, guides readers through 'knowing what is the right thing to do and finding the courage to do it.' His focus is on the business world, his style is lively and stimulating, illustrated with cartoons, and the book is sprinkled throughout with thought-provoking quotations.
7   In *Ethical Maturity in the Helping Professions: Making difficult life and work decisions*, Carroll asks what processes are involved in making ethical decisions and how do we, as humans, arrive at what we call morally or ethically good or bad decisions? The book reflects on the history, philosophy and science of ethics to provide a comprehensive overview of the most influential ideas in ethical thinking across the ages and consider the ethical challenges faced in various contexts of educational, research, business and organisational sectors.
8   See de Graaf and Levy (2011) for a full discussion of this approach to working as a coach or consultant in organisations.
9   In her article 'Minding the Gap: Ethical considerations for therapeutic engagement' (2011), Sue Eusden emphasises the nature and necessity of risk in the therapeutic relationship, often not well accounted for in ethics codes. She proposes that incidents that might be viewed by some as unethical are actually common in a relationship such as therapy and can be considered an essential part of the process. She further suggests that ethical practice involves 'minding the gap' between intention and outcome, which requires ongoing attention to interactions. We believe this applies equally to the supervision relationship.

Chapter 7

Supervision in practice

Courage and vulnerability

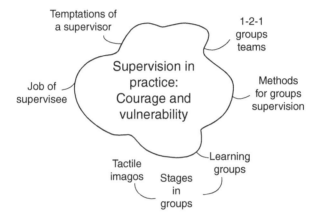

I realise there is something I do before I start a session; I let myself know that I am enough – not perfect, perfect wouldn't be enough – but that I am human, and that is enough. There is nothing this (person) can say or do or feel that I can't feel in myself.[1]

Practice is about the doing (and the 'not doing', which can be just as important). It is where theory and tools are transformed by the alchemy of a relationship into life-changing experiences – as the rubber of the relationship hits the road of learning – where the supervisor's own experience is tempered and tested by the reality of engaging with another.

Practice is about the saying. It is where each person engaged in the work needs to have the courage to be honest, the vulnerability to be brave and the willingness to sit empathically with another without judgement – and all this whilst accessing the intellectual capability to assess rigorously in the moment and articulate the validity of what is happening. Practice does indeed take practice!

And, in order to do the doing and say the saying, we have first to be immersed in the 'being': allowing ourselves to be vulnerable, to find our courage, to sit with the flawed reality of our own being – and that of the other. If we are to be truly vulnerable and courageous, we need to realise that we can only be as good as we are right now – that we cannot always be right; we do not have access to the ultimate truth. But, also, we can offer the best of ourselves – remembering that all that is asked of us is to be stronger and wiser *in the moment*. It is in developing our 'being' that we bring all of our capability, knowledge and experience to the doing.

A coach supervisee may have had experience of being coached by another coach, of peer-group discussion, or of reviewing their work with a coach mentor. All of these experiences may seem similar – and all of them will have value – so how is the practice of professional supervision different?

The temptations of a supervisor

Being in a supervision relationship means being subject to just the same invitations to psychological games as when we are in any other relationship. Hopefully, recognising what is happening – and resolving it – is also part of the supervision relationship, and provides useful data for the development of all concerned. However, there are some particular temptations in being a supervisor, including:

> Befriending – is perhaps even more tempting for the supervisor than the coach. After all, this is a relationship of mutual respect, equality and value (all which could be perfectly validly expected within a friendship), so it is very easy to become friends. Although supervision is generally a friendly relationship, it's not a friendship: it's a professional, contracted-for relationship with distinct roles, none of which should give way to the temptations of friendship.
>
> Being the Expert – it is so easy to be seduced out of our proper role by, 'I would love your wisdom on what you would do' or, 'Do something to help me: you're wonderful at this' or even by our own inner voice saying, 'I've been doing this for years, they want me to share everything I know, and they've come to me because they're out of their depth' – all being particular manifestations of the expert.
>
> The Trusted Advisor or Consultant – the most frustrating thing about this temptation is that people can't (or won't, or don't) take our advice! But, no matter how well you can see what they should do, they can only be 'them' – they can't be us. There's no point in telling them, even if they do invite us to, because people will not do something unless they make it their own. They can only be themselves – not their supervisor.
>
> The invitation to 'we' or 'us' – 'we're in this together': actually we're not – we're in this separately! Each of us has our own distinct role, and it is only in being separate, and bringing our separate minds to bear on the question before us, that we can harness the wisdom of all parties.

How do we stay out of these temptations? Two ideas:

Unattached intimacy

> Years ago – when I had already been a coach for a number of years, I was talking to a colleague about why I loved the work so much and why I seemed to be quite good at it – in fact I felt it really was 'the work I was born to do'! And he said, 'But of course; a good coach creates a relationship of unattached intimacy which, for you, is the most comfortable way to be in relationship with another.'

So, what is this 'unattached intimacy'? It connects directly to the question of why coaching and supervision are not the same as 'befriending' — unlike most of the other interpersonal relationships in our lives, with the possible exception of therapy. What we offer as coaches and supervisors is a special opportunity to be with another person in a very intimate way – where we are safe to truly be ourselves alongside someone who doesn't have an agenda for us and can let us have our 'separate minds'.

And, while this is true for both coaches and supervisors, I think it is particularly important when we are working as supervisors. Mutuality, courage, and a readiness for both disclosure and discomfort, are essential in supervision. It is possible to work very usefully as a coach without the client ever knowing what we are feeling, but to be effective as a supervisor we share our own feelings, understand where they belong, and use them in the service of learning for the whole system. This is 'unattached intimacy'.

The value of silence

> Indeed, so important is silence that permission to speak should seldom be granted even to mature disciples, no matter how good or holy or constructive their talk.[2]

This quotation from the Rule of St Benedict may seem extreme, but is worth reflecting on: it is in the silences that a supervision session may be most alive, as each participant lets their inner awareness generate, if not answers, at least some indications of direction. The temptations above are all temptations to talking: filling the space without addressing what needs to be addressed.

Silence can mean many things – anxiety, puzzlement, uncertainty, resistance or protection – but it can also mean recognition of something profound, a joy in discovery and a sense of liberation. So, whether in a pair or a group, all silences need sensitive, discerning attention from the supervisor. Silence in a group can be an indication of some tension in the dynamic between members or, beautifully but perhaps less often, reveal a shared deep appreciation and insight.

With all the above in mind, let's turn now to practical questions about what happens in supervision:

What do we do?

Supervision may be one-to-one or in groups (usually of four to six coaches), and it may be funded by the individual coaches or their organisations. Whether you are a supervisor or a supervisee, there are a number of things to consider when deciding to work one-to-one or in a group. As you read our descriptions, it will become clear that there are both similarities and differences between these two methods. For example, the contract between supervisor and supervisee(s) will need to be set up and managed differently, but right from the start the same consideration is given to supervisees' levels of education and experience. 'No assumptions' is probably the watchword here!

As you read the following story, think about what you would have done.

A supervisor's story:

> This happened in Stacey's first supervision session with a relatively inexperienced coach:
>
> Five minutes before the end of their time, the coach said, 'By the way, I've landed my first piece of work in an organisation! I'll be a consultant for them, I'm coaching their Head of HR and the seven members of their sales team – starting next week.'
>
> 'Wow,' Stacey said, 'that must have been quite a complex contract to sort out. How did the three-way contracting meetings go?'
>
> 'The what?' the coach replied.

Unpick this story from different points of view:

- Is this primarily a management, support or development issue?
- What ethical issues are there?
- Where would you start?
- How do you enable a coach to know what to bring to supervision?
- How do you deal with incidents like this – sometimes known as 'doorknob issues' or, 'By the way, Doctor'?

Supervision one-to-one

One-to-one supervision is often the choice of the experienced, busy coach who will want time to explore a number of their own particular client issues in addition to attending to other aspects of their increasingly well-developed identity. They may be seeking a higher level of input from the supervisor in one particular area. The greater level of exposure of the supervisee and the supervisor in a one-to-one relationship can be incredibly rewarding – but also challenging when there is no respite from it being 'all about us'.

Although the ideal is to meet in person, much supervision is done by phone or online. When supervisor and coach are working at some distance from each other (maybe in different countries), a good combination is to have regular – even if not frequent – face-to-face meetings, with phone or e-sessions in between.

Supervisors will be drawing on many skill-sets. They usually possess a range of professional expertise – coaching certainly, maybe counselling or therapy, management, consultancy, teaching, mentoring or advocacy. At different stages in supervision, depending on their level of experience and development, the coach may want to access the supervisor's knowledge of a particular situation. Sometimes this may be appropriate, sometimes not; ideally, the supervisor will discern what is a real need and what might be an invitation to 'Do it (i.e. the thinking) for me' – or, 'Just tell me what to do!'

Figure 7.1 shows the continuum[3] of roles that a supervisor may take up, depending on the coach's level of experience and the requirement of the moment. The 'pathway' between them is contracting and, as indicated, there are sets of interventions (to tell, teach, mentor, challenge, co-work), and any one of these can be contracted-for within a supervision session.

The contract is the 'container' that holds and allows the development of a safe and free relationship. Supervisor and coach will have made an overall contract covering how they work together. As each session starts, they will agree the agenda and whether a contract is needed for the whole session. They will also, of course, be contracting for each piece of work as they go.

Many coaches are resistant to contracting with their clients but, without a good contract, there is a real danger of coach and client just having a chat. If you want to end up somewhere – you need to know where you're going! Once contracting has been well modelled in supervision, it can become easy and elegant for the coach to bring it into the coach-client encounter as well: often, for the client as for the

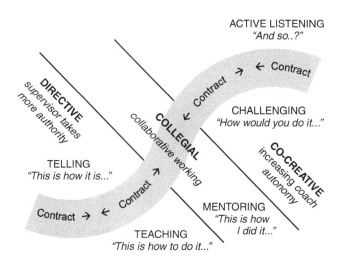

Figure 7.1 Contracting continuum.

coach-supervisee, the contract really is the work. As a client, the process of getting really clear about what you want, why this particular relationship will help you achieve it and how you will know once you have – often means your next steps are self-evident and easily taken. Contracting in coaching also gives the client a wonderful experience of really thinking for themselves, being able to get clear and to problem solve in the company of another – but without being told or advised (however knowledgeable or well-intended that advisor may be). In supervision we often find ourselves asking, 'So what was the contract?' Sometimes, we wonder if we should simply cut to the chase and ask this question at the beginning of each piece of supervision – since it's probably where we will end up!

So, as supervisors we need to model good contracting and re-contracting with our supervisees. A typical session might follow this shape:

- What has the supervisee brought to today's session?
- What is the order of importance?
- What are we looking for in terms of outcomes?
- What particularly does the coach want from me, the supervisor?

At this point the supervisor may be silently asking themselves:

- Is there a thread here?
- Have I heard this before from this coach?

And then:

- Are either of us noticing any patterns here?

Or even:

- What am I, the supervisor, experiencing as I hear this? Am I being transparent in sharing my experience and feelings?
- Is there a parallel process operating?
- Is the personal intruding into the professional? If it is, then can we deal with it here or is it something the coach needs to take somewhere else (maybe to their own coach, mentor-coach, counsellor or therapist)?

This leads on to talking together about:

- 'Understanding what we understand': how does this relate specifically to the context of the work the coach is doing?
- What are they going to do now that's different?
- How are they going to assess the impact and value of the difference?
- How are they feeling about this session, what have they learnt?
- How are they feeling about themselves?

And, over time, as part of the 'bigger picture', the supervisor will be asking whether the coach is learning and developing:

- in competence?
- in confidence?
- in self-awareness (self-supervision)?

Also:

- Are they noticing what's changing for them?
- Am I seeing the coach's self-recognition in the moment? Is there less 'doing' and more 'being'?
- Are they developing an increasingly clear identity as a coach?
- Is there a sense of OK-ness? Or – if I'm feeling uncomfortable – why?

Client list review

It is useful to have a regular review of the supervisee's entire client list:

- Who on it seems to get all the attention in supervision – and why?
- Who never seems to be brought to supervision – and why?
- Are there any patterns?
- Are some clients so 'easy', they don't seem to need reflection, and why might that be? For example, might the coach be colluding?
- Or, do they only ever bring the problem-clients, and are they not using supervision to celebrate and learn from all that is going well?
- Are you as supervisor introducing a bias to what the coach feels they should be bringing to supervision?
- Is there anything in your beliefs or behaviours which suggests to the coach that some topics are not OK – or even not safe?
- If the supervisee coaches both one-to-one and in teams or groups, do they bring all of the work – or only some?

Supervision in groups

Group supervision can be a great place to work if all the coaches are novices or not doing a lot of coaching, as a group provides the opportunity to 'piggy-back' on other people's stories. There may also be significant value in noticing that, for instance, 'I'm not alone' in finding something difficult. Belonging in a supportive group of learners who celebrate each other's growth can accelerate a coach's confidence and development. Noticing how other coaches work, the issues they bring, their difference from 'me', can help the developing coach form their particular identity as a coach (it can also be more economically viable for a low-earning coach).

Of course, group supervision also includes the dynamic of a developing group – which needs a different kind of care from a one-to-one relationship. Below, we consider what is involved in leading a group through its development – along with some of the potential tensions of group work.

The coaches in the group may never have had supervision; even if they have, it may not have been in the way you do it. It can be helpful to start with a half-day workshop in which you 'teach' some of the models you will be using and agree an initial contract – for example, will everyone always be there, or will the group change its constituent parts each time? And how frequently will they meet?

A typical session might follow this pattern:

- Check-in for each member – including the supervisor;
- How am I – right now?
- Things that stand out for me since the last session, in terms of learning, concern, celebration;
- What do I bring today?
- What do I want from today?

There may be an established pattern that enables a mix of short and long supervision sessions, or the group may decide how they want each session to run. There may be a contract in place that the supervisee chooses the method, or this may be decided on the day by the whole group. Some groups may feel that everyone must 'have a go' – others that the key themes that emerged in the check-in can be addressed more fully by one or two members being supervised and the learning taken by all. Time needs to be made at the end for a brief check-out.

However, 'group supervision' can mean different things: some supervisors expect to do one-to-one supervision, with each participant having a share of the time and the rest of the group being observers, perhaps offering observations or feedback at the end of each piece. This may be your regular format, but it is not the only way. It can also be worthwhile to invite all the group to be involved more meaningfully by taking part in the actual process of the supervision: this promotes learning at many levels, and supports the development of all the members through trying out their intuition, thinking and reflective practice.

Here are some possibilities for working with the whole group together, with one person each time as the 'focus' for the learning. As always, it is important to contract for the piece, and this will include how the central person intends to involve the group and, as they get to know the various activities, choose which one suits them best at this moment. Some of these methods for group supervision need to be handled with care – we have included health warnings below – and the 'official' supervisor will in all cases be holding and containing the process for the protection of all the participants.

Methods for group supervision

Most of these are suitable for any group, though the sophistication of the supervisees – in terms of their technical competence and their experience as coaches, their emotional intelligence and their robustness as group members – needs to be taken into account when choosing the method. A rule of thumb is that, early in a group's formation or with a group whose membership changes each time, the lead supervisor needs to retain more of the control and management of the process, whereas, once a group is well established and trusting, the members can take more of the control and management and, very typically, the supervisee will elect to choose the method. (See also below, 'Leadership and group development in supervision groups'.)

In these approaches to group supervision, it is important that one person, normally the 'official' supervisor, is leading and holding the process; that they clearly describe the method, especially if it is unfamiliar, and contract for all the roles, including any specific observations. We also suggest that after any of these methods is used, a 'process review' is done to help to embed the learning.

One-to-one supervision in the group

With others silent but observing, this can be followed by a process review, by a time of people reporting on their own learning, or by feedback and strokes to the supervisee presenting. Whichever method is used, it should be clearly contracted with the group before the start of the work.

Suggestion circle

The coach presents their issue or dilemma for supervision and each group member then makes a single suggestion or asks a single question. The supervisee then chooses which one to follow up. Afterwards, the whole group can share the thinking that led to their suggestions or questions – or not, if the presenting coach feels they have gained what they need already. (*Health warning*: those whose suggestions or questions aren't followed up need to remain in Adult, neither discounting their own value nor feeling discounted by the supervisee!.)

Observation and feedback

The groups' observations can be general or specific – members can be asked to look out for language, incongruities, discounts etc., or to say what they notice about the whole piece.

Playing tapes

A group member plays a short section of a recorded coaching session which they have pre-selected as being in some way curious, interesting, confusing – or even typical. The supervisee may ask the group to listen for specific points, e.g. questions or moving forward, or to share anything that seemed significant. Alternatively, the group may choose something specific that they have identified as a current learning point for them all.

Process review

This follows a piece of supervision (of any type). It is a time to reflect on the process, it's effectiveness, the learning gained, to ask questions of the supervisor about their thinking. It is not a way of doing 'extra' supervision! The supervisor needs to keep the focus on process, not content.

Sharing responses

Once the coach has told their story, the group share whatever it evoked for each – an emotion, a picture, a metaphor or sensation. This is a good way of 'outing' parallel process: what is happening that is out of the coach's awareness?

By reporting their experience of hearing about a stuck situation with a client, group members draw attention to the process – through their somatic experience or by reporting the images and words evoked. Responses should be directed to the supervisor, not the coach, to avoid overload. (*Health warning*: you may have a group member who says they 'don't do metaphor or emotion' and gets quite upset ('emotional'!). To preempt this happening in a new group, it may be worth testing the idea before actually doing it: if it does happen, beware of the group jumping in and collectively coaching the group member to help them understand why they have this 'problem'.)

Pause button

This can be used in several ways. If there are two supervisors, the one who is working can 'press pause' while they share their thinking with their colleague or check out why they feel stuck; or a group member can be the supervisor, and 'pause' to consult an experienced leader; or the whole group can 'pause' the process for checking and questioning (for experienced groups only). This is particularly useful in peer group supervision for supervisors, or where there is an agreed contract with an experienced group of coaches who are seeking to increasingly self- or peer-supervise.

Baton

The supervisee first presents their supervision 'issue'. All the group participate, either by 'passing the baton' every 2 minutes, or by a signal that someone wants to pick up on an intervention. A variation is 'doubling', where one person is the supervisor and others can take over for a few minutes by moving to stand behind the supervisor and 'be' them. This is good for practice in groups where members are already – or are becoming – supervisors themselves.

Listening in

A supervisee presents their 'situation', then stays silent while the group discusses what they have heard – with an agreement that everybody will stay OK-OK. Afterwards, the presenter 'rejoins' the group and says what has been useful. This is a good method for preventing games of 'Yes, but …'. Alternatively, it is a wonderfully validating exercise to use when the supervisee knows that a piece of work has somehow, mysteriously, gone really well – but doesn't understand what their contribution was to it! The group can help to reveal it to them. (*Health warning*: this should only be done with a healthy, well-established group. If the supervisee has presented something difficult or challenging for them, they can easily go to a not-OK place as they listen to the discussion. It is really important that the frame and content of the conversation remains enquiring, rather than judging. As a way of enhancing safety, it's a good idea to have the supervisor sit with the supervisee while the rest of the group have their discussion. The two of them can then take a little time to review what the supervisee has heard and how they have framed it – which may be somewhat different from how the supervisor has done – before both returning to the group.)

Role-play

The coach who is presenting role-plays the client with whom they feel stuck or have some difficulty; someone else plays them (i.e. the coach). The presenter then reports which interventions were effective in moving them on.

Mapping

The eight-eyed model can provide a very powerful exercise when used in a group. A coach presents their 'problem' and is supervised by another group member, with each of the other members observing the attention given to one of the eight areas of the model. Everyone then reports in turn what they have observed. Discussion can be focused on any of the areas or the connections between them.

Cascade

This is only for experienced or supervisors' peer-supervision groups. Someone brings a coaching dilemma for supervision and is supervised by a member of the group. The supervisor then presents this piece of work for supervision by another member of the group, who in turn receives supervision from another – or from the leading supervisor. The cascade can be longer in more experienced groups.

It is very effective, and sometimes dramatic, if only the first two members of the cascade (i.e. coach and supervisor) are in the room initially, and each subsequent supervisor only enters when it is their turn to do the work. This is a wonderful way of seeing parallel process in operation. There is an example of this in Chapter 2. (*Health warning*: the coach bringing the dilemma may feel isolated as the focus moves away from them – so remember to come back to them at the end to check out what they have gained from all the discussion. The example story shows how this can happen.)

Sculpt/tactile imago/constellation

These are all variations for 'imaging' the supervision situation. With sculpting, the presenter places people to represent the situation, then considers what can be learnt; similarly in a constellation, the experience of the participants provides previously unrecognised material. A tactile imago serves to represent the situation, while also giving new information.

Tactile imagos

Tactile imagos[4] are a very effective way of showing us our own mental picture of a group or organisation. They are more effective than drawing because they really are tactile and flexible – you can keep moving the pieces around until the image seems right. They share with sculpting and constellation work the sense of clarity that creating something visual brings.

Think of a group you are part of – maybe as a supervisor or as part of a team or peer group. It might be a group where you are aware that something is not quite right. Start with a piece of plain paper and some stones and/or shells (we travel with boxes of shells and stones). Take time to look and feel as you choose some to represent you, your team, group, contacts or colleagues. Then place them on the paper to picture the group as feels like an accurate representation to you. In Figure 7.2(a), 'me' seems to feel close to some team members and more distant from others; one person may be experienced as 'prickly', and the boss is more or less separate from the rest of the team.

The exercise works well when done with a partner who can ask questions or simply witness your thinking process – or else you can each do it simultaneously and discuss as you go: the energy level is usually high! You may want to move the items around or change them, experimenting until the imago seems to fit your sense of the group. Take your time.

When you have created your 'present' tactile imago and talked with your partner, think about how you would like the group to be in the future: move the stones and shells around, change them for others, whatever you want. Work towards your desired imago and talk it through together. Then ask yourself what needs to happen to bring this about. In Figure 7.2(b) some personnel are new (or maybe new aspects of the same people) and some have been moved into different configurations.

When you are observing your partner creating a tactile imago, avoid interpreting or putting your own slant on what you see – the power of this technique lies in each person deciding their own meaning. Tactile imagos can be a speedy way of revealing problems or blocks in groups and teams. They are also a great tool for supervision, both in groups and one-to-one.

As an exercise, use the tactile imago to model a group you lead as a supervisor or, if you've not yet led a group, one to which you belong.

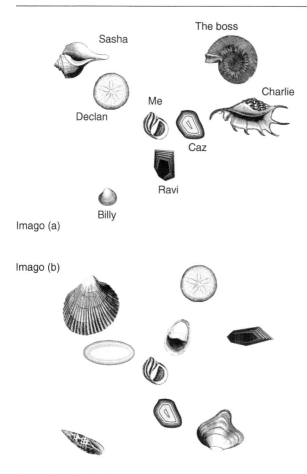

Imago (a)

Imago (b)

Figure 7.2 Tactile imagos.

Leadership and group development in supervision groups

As a supervisor, leading a supervision group is something you may or may not want to do – and of course this may change over time. In addition to all of those things you need to be aware of when supervising an individual, there is also the dynamic of the group itself and its relationships – with you as the supervisor, with one another as individuals, and with the whole group as an entity. And all of these will change over time. Below is some useful information about how groups form and grow, and the role of the leader in that process.

Looking at each of the stages of a group in turn, we will consider what the supervisor's enabling attitudes and actions need to be to help a group (and each individual within it) move towards self-realisation and autonomy.

Petruska Clarkson explored such issues in detail, listing empowering and dis-empowering behaviours that leaders may exhibit in groups.[5] Our emphasis here is on groups whose primary task is supervision, so we will concentrate on realistic aims for supervisors.

Each of us has a 'leader' slot within our own imago, either with information about ourselves as leaders or about leaders we have known. We may feel a need to model our behaviour to suit a fantasised or remembered supervisor, and this may give rise to difficulties if this figure is not appropriate to our current situation.

Before reading further, you might like to refer back to the material about group imagos in Chapter 2 and re-acquaint yourself with the four stages.

Stage 1: Imagine

In the first stage, when the group is forming and participants' imagos are as in Figure 2.8(a), the supervisor needs to be aware of their own imago and any anxi-eties it may bring up for them. A clear structure and an open approach will help healthy group formation (Table 7.1).

Table 7.1 Leader behaviours (a)

Enabling behaviours	Disabling behaviours
Clearly stating task and purpose of group	Confusion about task and purpose
Contracting clearly about expectations of self and members	Mixed messages about 'who does what'
Give information about times, venue etc.	Lack of information
Arrange room appropriately for group	Poor housekeeping
Provide overview	Secrecy
Allow time for group to get to know each other	Anxiety to 'get on with' supervision
Take responsibility for structure and protection	Lack structure, too 'laissez-faire'
Model OK-OK respect and interest	Appear 'one-up' or agitated

Adapted from Napper and Newton 2000, p. 10.12.

Table 7.2 Leader behaviours (b)

Enabling behaviours	Disabling behaviours
Listens to criticism and responds from OK position	Persecutes by denying viewpoints or taking sides
Maintains OK–OK perspective	Ignores conflict or smooths it over
Affirms individual's ideas and responses	'Pleases' or 'tries hard' to make things right
Flexible within boundaries of task, maintains structure	Marshmallows or acts rigid
Negotiates changes in procedure and methods	Says 'must be done this way'

Adapted from Napper and Newton 2000, p. 10.13.

The importance of good contracting is obvious. This is what enables a group to make a good start, so that participants feel powerful, interested and excited about the task.

Stage 2: Meeting

In the second stage too, Figure 2.8(b), the leader may need to handle negative feelings of the group – which can show up as conflict or rebellion (for example, 'Why do we have to do it this way?') or less obviously as low energy, passivity or no enthusiasm for joining in. This is the time of testing the supervisor's competence for the job, so modelling authenticity and flexibility are key – annoying as it may feel at the time (Table 7.2).

While this stage is going on, we may need to get support from colleagues – in order to avoid blaming ourselves as everything appears to go wrong!

Stage 3: Angling

In the third stage, Figure 2.8(c), each person in the group will be working out how they stand with the leader: who is the 'star coach', bringing something every time; who challenges most effectively; who 'hides' in the group. So the supervisor may still be holding negativity, and still be being blamed or criticised, but now the group settles with each member beginning to feel comfortable with their own imago as they play out familiar patterns of behaviour (Table 7.3).

This stage goes better when there is affirmation built-in for everyone in the group and recognition of each member's contribution.

The key at this stage is to model flexibility and encouragement, so that healthy norms can develop. We may be drawing on our own recollections of supervisors we have known. This can be made a useful tool by asking 'What do I have stored in my Parent which can help me be an effective supervisor here?'

Table 7.3 Leader behaviours (c)

Enabling behaviours	Disabling behaviours
Facilitates development of group's unique culture and identity	Has preconceived ideas of group's identity
Respects group and individual members	Makes inflexible rules without negotiation
Makes clear own values and stance	Does not challenge destructive behaviour from members
Maintains flexibility	Expects all groups to be the same

Adapted from Napper and Newton 2000, p. 10.13.

Stage 4: Getting On

As the fourth stage begins, Figure 2.8(d), there will be a sense of closeness, of the leader being seen as a real person (not a 'Supervision Guru'), and therefore they will be able to relax and let the group happen, with members taking on more self-directed learning and sharing responsibility for the group's development. At this stage, some of the methods for more experienced groups provide opportunities for challenge and rapid development (Table 7.4).

Ending the group

As the end of the group's time together comes into view, the leader needs to be clear about completing the task without a sense of loss getting in the way. This may mean once again containing the group's negative feelings, particularly if there is an unrealistic desire for the group to continue.

The 'holding' role can be especially hard if the leader themselves feels the loss. Rituals can help here, as people have opportunities to say what has been good for them and say 'Goodbye', not just to each other but to the whole experience of being a member of the group (Table 7.5).

Table 7.4 Leader behaviours (d)

Enabling behaviours	Disabling behaviours
Lets individuals and group 'get on with it'	Holds on to leader role
Shares leadership appropriately	Controls group – invites adaptive behaviour
Maintains structure and focus as needed	Expects group to conform to their picture
Invites exploration and experiment	Doesn't listen to other ideas
Offers permissions, encouragement and strokes	Enjoins 'one way' to do things
Becomes a resource	Has 'right' idea where group is going
Is a real person in the group	Models and invites game-playing

Adapted from Napper and Newton 2000, p. 10.14.

Table 7.5 Leader behaviours (e)

Enabling behaviours	Disabling behaviours
Creates space for group and individuals to grieve	Rushes endings so no time for rituals or feelings
Keeps to finishing time	Allows unclear finish, e.g. no agreed time
Gives time for group 'story'	Denies 'downs' in reminiscing
Gives appropriate feedback	Rescues by unrealistic reassurance

Adapted from Napper and Newton 2000, p. 10.15.

Curiously, endings seem to be difficult right through the chain: for clients with their coaches; for coaches with their supervisors; and right back down the other way. Maybe 'blurring endings' is such a well-embedded process in our culture that we have never properly learnt how to do it.

This key competence can be modelled and learnt within the supervision relationship. In Chapter 2, we wrote about contracting for how the group will deal with any difficulties that arise between its members right at the beginning – designing into the work ways of addressing these. The way of ending should also be discussed up-front: how everyone feels about endings, 'What we need to know that will help us to do it well'. In this way, both (or all) parties are acknowledging that the relationship will end and that its ending can be discussed, negotiated, and achieved.

> One coach we know prides himself on having great endings with his clients: he celebrates and enjoys their completion of the work and they both cheerfully walk away. And he then maintains a semi – or completely – social relationship with nearly all of them for years.

- How do you feel about this way of working?
- How do you manage endings?
- Are there relationships in your life that have actually ended, but where this hasn't been acknowledged – or do you usually move on?
- When you do make endings, are they graceful or painful?
- How does this show up in your work?
- How would you like it to be?

Supervision in organisations

This may involve one-to-one supervision of coaches (and so be a similar process to any other supervision relationship), or it may be with a group of coaches as part of an organisational system. Internal coaches often have had a limited amount of training, so you may need to spend a lot more time at the 'telling' end of the contracting continuum (Figure 7.1) – refreshing skills through revising competencies, observing group members coaching each other or picking up themes in the situations they bring for supervision, and so on. They may also only be coaching for a few hours each month, so will not always have 'stuff' to bring.

As suggested earlier, when internal coaches have never had supervision before, it may be a good idea to start with a half-day workshop where you 'teach' some of the models you will be using, make clear agreements about expectations, and so on.

Supervising in-house coaches may also mean taking account of potential ethical issues connected with their loyalties or conflicts within the organisation (we explored some of these in Chapter 6).

When we encounter an organisational culture we are unfamiliar with, or realise that there are different agendas at work, applying our ethical principles and following our decided-on procedures can sometimes be challenging.

The supervisor needs to be aware of the interpersonal dynamics of the group and the development of the group culture. There are a number of models for understanding what happens in groups – and the stages a group may go through, from formation to ending. The group imagos model (described above and in Chapter 2) can provide a useful framework for your awareness of group process and dynamics. It will make group supervision an exciting and perceptive experience – particularly when group members come to share that awareness and so gain personal insights for growth and professional development.

Contracting for group supervision will include:

- ways of negotiating how much time each participant gets;
- the boundaries of the group; how people join and leave;
- who the supervisor is responsible to: what level of confidentiality members expect;
- who is responsible for 'admin'?

Clear contracting will reduce the potential for competition and the anxiety that can arise around being 'seen' as a supervisee. Also, the task of the group needs to be stated – is it entirely task-focused or will time be given to process and personal needs? The group supervisor manages considerable complexity!

All of the above implies a group that meets together in order to get supervision of coaching (or supervision of supervision). A team, on the other hand, has an existence outside the group; this means that, while the supervisor still needs to monitor the culture and dynamics, there will be additional factors to consider, such as:

- Boundaries: who is included, and what working relationships do they have outside this group?
- Role confusion: if people at different levels of management are part of an internal coaching team, does the team itself need supervision – as well as supervision of work with clients?

A team has its own dynamic (its norms, its members' expectations of each other) which will be apparent in supervision, but may or may not be up for discussion and negotiation. This may be brought into team members' awareness at the contracting stage, as an opportunity for potential team development.

> Lee was working as Team Coach with a high-energy customer services team in an organisation going through re-structuring. There was some dispute between two members, one of them quite aggressive, which was affecting the rest of the team – many mentioned it in their personal contact with Lee as well as it being apparent when they all meet together. The Director was not sympathetic when

Lee tried to discuss the situation with him, thinking that everyone should 'just get on with the job'. As part of the contract all the team had been offered one-to-one coaching but the aggressive team member had not taken up this opportunity.

What could Lee do? If you were Lee's supervisor how would you approach this when it is brought to supervision?

The job of the supervisee

We've described a lot of what the supervisor does and is responsible for, but we've also said that this is a collegial, co-created and co-contracted relationship – so what are the supervisees' responsibilities, what do they themselves need to be bringing to the table?[6]

Keep coming to supervision

This may seem obvious but it is important. To be accountable to the profession and to the professional commitment of supervision is the first step. If you have doubts about supervision, air them and share in resolving them. Then agree how often you will meet and keep to it.

Participate

Whether in an individual supervision partnership or in a group: take an equal part in creating the beginning contract and maintaining it; be an active member in the relationship(s); don't coast or be a passenger; reflect on your work, in real-time in the group or with your supervisor.

Prepare

Arrive knowing what you want to address, even if you haven't fully formulated it – and the clearer you can be, the more likely you are to get what you need; make (and keep) whatever notes are helpful to you, looking back over them at intervals and always before annual or bi-annual reviews.

Be open

Make use of supervision and learn from others' supervision too. Give any information that seems part of the story, even if you are not sure how, and be authentic in your responses to feedback and interventions.

Share

… in relationships by being real and honest, giving feedback, support and encouragement to others in the group, bringing examples of how you have used supervision and how it has made a difference; celebrate your own and others' growth and successes.

Take responsibility

Don't expect to be told, advised or directed: accept challenges to your actions or thinking; believe in your own and others' autonomy and capacity to problem-solve.

Keep growing

As you develop, the things you bring to supervision will change: don't try to hold on to previous stages; as you grow, check with yourself before a session if you really need to bring each item – or if you already have the answer.

> One coach contracted with himself to stop on his way to a session, go through his list and tick-off items he could self-supervise – and then report on his successful analysis and decisions. And then, of course, he had more time for supervision on the items he really needed to work on with his supervisor.

Use what you learn

... firstly to improve your service to clients; but also to enhance the coaching profession; to encourage colleagues; and maybe to think about becoming a supervisor yourself.

And, for everyone concerned – supervisors and supervisees, individually or as part of a group – we can all keep in mind the words of Carl Rogers: 'Not perfect ... but human; and that is enough'.

> We meet: two heads together
> A puzzle
> A startle
> A laugh
> An understanding
> A wondering
> A noticing
> A step forward
> A look back
> A laugh
> Well done us![7]

Notes

1   Carl Rogers, cited in Rachel Naomi Remen *'The Search for Healing'* in R. Carlson and B. Shield (eds) *'Healers on Healing'* (Los Angeles: Tarcher, 1989, p. 93).
2   *Rule of St Benedict*, Chapter 6, 'Restraint of Speech'.

3 The diagram, Figure 7.1, was developed by a group of internal coach supervisors at Fujitsu – many thanks to all of them for allowing us to use it here, albeit with some changes to widen its application.

4 Building on Berne's idea of group imagos, and also on related 'imaging' models, Doug Hampson developed the notion of tactile imagos (Hampson 1998). Shells, pebbles, stones and other small items can be used, and they should be tactile – both looking and feeling are significant to people choosing one to 'be' a group or team member. The tactile imago was created by Doug as a way of understanding the stages in the life of a group and how group members perceive them.

5 Petruska Clarkson related the stages of group development as described by Berne and by Tuckman (forming, storming, norming, performing) to the changing role of the leader as the group moves on (Clarkson 1992). She was thinking of therapy groups, but her ideas apply equally to learning groups and supervision groups, since the characteristic phases are the same for any kind of group. In 'Tactics', Napper and Newton adapted Clarkson's charts, and we have further adapted them here. This material is taken from Tactics (Napper & Newton) and adapted for coach supervision groups.

6 An excellent guide to being a supervisee is 'On Being a Supervisee' by Michael Carroll and Maria Gilbert (2005). It is also useful for supervisors! It is written for all helping and talking professions, and thoroughly covers all aspects of being a supervisee.

7 Thanks to Delscey Burns.

Reflections – what next?

Setting out

When we first thought of writing this book, we had an idea about what it would be: we'd take what we had already done in our supervision 'manual' and turn it into a slim paperback, with maybe a bit more 'wrapping' about our thinking and why we do things our way.

But we soon discovered that we really do 'make the road by walking', and this walking was creating a new road that went further than we had expected – and with a few more turnings along the way.

One of the reasons for this change was that, in writing together and sharing our developing thoughts with colleagues as we went on, we were engaged in the same process that we wanted to demonstrate in the book: co-creative working – being open to things unexpectedly new.

An important change of direction was in how we thought about our readership: surely our ideas about supervision would apply in any kind of human relations work, counselling, therapy, social work or consultancy – not only to coaching, the field where we had first promoted them? So, we should be addressing supervisors in general.

But coaching occupies a unique place in the landscape of supervision: many clients, many coaches also, would not see themselves as primarily concerned in their own personal development, but in becoming more effective in their professional context. This makes for a different slant in coach supervision: we realised we had become part of an 'interpretive community' of people who were involved in making our discoveries available, getting what we do and how we do it codified and 'out there' in a way that made it accessible and available.

Our 'walking' has not been a linear progression; nor is the way in which coaches and supervisors become increasingly capable and assured over time. We start down a path, explore its byways; maybe set off in a new direction, get lost and then eventually return to our original path – or rediscover it by chance, and remember what a good path it was. You may have found this out for yourself as you read: some things made absolute and practical sense to you straight away – others only came into focus much later on.

Landmarks

On looking back along that path, there are some recurring themes:

- The centrality of experiential, personal learning as the intention of supervision.
- The importance and worth of relational working – seeing things afresh through being with others.
- The value of being part of a co-creative community of practice.
- The place of discourse in creating meaning and a common language.
- Story, narrative and metaphor as the way we all communicate and how we all develop.
- The significance of a positive psychology that is focused on growth and thriving.
- The necessity – and vitality – of bringing the whole self to the work.

Ways not taken

And, there are some landmarks that we have not chosen to attend to, signposts to pathways we have decided not to take. Two of these are significant, and might well point in directions we should explore in the future.

One is neuroscience – currently a dominant topic and the subject of many enticing claims about coaching as well as learning. To explore with any meaning its relevance to supervision would take us outside our territory and into areas we feel doubtful about. Although 'neuro-everything' is touted as a cure for many social ills, on closer examination it is often the metaphors derived from these ideas that are cited as effective, rather than the science itself. Neuromyths abound; so we decided to leave this turning unexplored.

Another, more regretted, omission is research. There is not a great deal of research on coach supervision – beyond how much it is accessed and by whom. This is fruitful territory for future exploration: the first stage being 'what works' and how do we know that? The further reaches being, how and why are some approaches or interventions effective? What do we prioritise – usefulness, outcomes, personal growth or whatever? Much data is available at the level of experience and anecdote; how do we move this on to become evidence – and decide what more we want to find out? We hope it will not be long before this field is well-populated and adding to the richness of the landscape around coach supervision.

Who we met

Along the way there have been many companions. Some of these relationships have endured for decades as we have continued to learn together; others, of immense and lasting significance, for now are in abeyance; several that were dormant have popped back to life as we discover similar paths chosen. Some directions we have decided on because a companion along the way pointed out an aspect of the scenery we had barely noticed.

Two final stories will illustrate what we mean:

A few years ago, I (Trudi) was asked to write something about why I write. This request made me think, and this led me to discover some things I had not been sufficiently aware of. One is that, partly, I write because I read, voraciously; words are important to me because words are the way we construct our lives – and our narratives. But, in the process of writing, I also need to be in dialogue with others. So, when I have an idea to write about, I generally take it to somewhere I can try it out – to a workshop or a peer group – and discuss it with other people until I feel clearer about it.

As the writing starts to take shape, I continue the discussion by sharing it with others to get their responses and opinions. By sharing what I want to say, I make myself open to what others want to say to me. All these ideas are gifts that get passed around and transformed as they travel. When I get to hear about how readers have developed my ideas, added to or critiqued them, or just liked what they read, the process of writing comes more alive for me.

What I write is not fiction, but the process is very similar to telling a story – or rather, sharing a story with others, and then joining with them in creating a new one.

After that article about writing appeared, a colleague emailed me, describing it as a gift that had opened his eyes to a new way of seeing. In his usual way of writing, he said, he saw himself as addressing an imaginary audience, but unmindful of developing a relationship with them. He began to realise that he was, perhaps, telling a story with an expected conclusion – rather than building a story together with others.[1]

So, why do I write? To engage with others, to share ideas, experiences and beliefs; to be part of the discourse in that interpretive community; to make a difference ... but my writing is only ever 'what will do for the moment', no idea is ever finished with or finalised.

And another story

I (Hilary) was having one of our regular catch-ups with a colleague, when she asked me 'given where you are in your career, why are you bothering to write a book?' Why am I? Whilst the thinking and collegial conversations we have are fascinating, stimulating and fun, it takes a lot of time and energy – and writing is in no way a passion for me. Nor do I have a desire to evangelise.

But this question really made me think: I know it matters to me to share the 'why, what and how' of our work, because I want people to learn in ways that are generative, restorative and fun. I want to help people to know that each of us has our own story, our own unique way of learning, that we can discover most effectively when we are in a supportive environment with others. I want our voice to join with the voices of all those other explorers who feel the same way: who teach, assess and supervise in safe, supportive – and challenging – relationships.

Signposts for the future

There are a few signposts that can be seen clearly. One points towards the increasing acceptance of supervision as important, indeed essential, in confirming the professionalisation of coaching. How can we encourage coaches and coaching associations to make it part of everyone's continuing development?

Another signpost indicates the need for grounded research on how all varieties of supervision are experienced and what makes them constructive and beneficial. And, a third suggests more sharing of insights on relational working between supervision in coaching and in other fields, such as counselling and therapy. We already learn from each other and we could do more.

So, this has changed from the book we thought we would be writing. On the journey to what we have written, we have not only gathered together new stories and new thinking – and created a wider discussion on supervision – we have also recognised how this work, and the way we aim to do it, will continue to be a part of the development of the coaching profession.

We know we don't have all the answers, but we hope we have brought something into the story of coach supervision: being resourceful, being OK with uncertainty, and being sufficient – for the moment!

Note

1 Thanks to Leonard Campos.

Competencies for coach supervision

Recently, a number of coaching associations have developed competencies for coach supervisors:

- The European Mentoring and Coaching Council (EMCC) have guidelines for supervision on their websites (www.emccouncil.org and www.emc-cuk.org) and, at the time of writing, are in the process of creating specific competencies.
- The Association for Coaching (www.associationforcoaching.com) have an excellent Supervision Principles Framework which is relational and 'psychological minded' in its approach to coach supervision.
- APECS, the Association for Professional Executive Coaching and Supervision (www.apecs.org) have guidelines for Supervisor Accreditation.

Hawkins and Smith (2006, p. 206) distinguish between

- *competencies* (the ability to use a skill);
- *capabilities* (the ability to use skills appropriately); and
- *capacities* (personal qualities).

The first two are about 'doing'; the latter is about 'being' (how we are with others and with ourselves). Hawkins and Smith summarise capacity as 'an internal spaciousness that enables total presence and the containing of complexity'. Although we continue to use the term competencies because of its wide application, and because it is in general use in coaching associations, we think the outline below (derived from many discussions with colleagues and debates on coach supervisor training courses) expresses the *capacities* of a relational coach supervisor.

We have organised the items into categories: firstly an overview of what can be expected of a coach supervisor throughout the relationship, then three sections corresponding to the three functions of supervision.

At the end of each section are some suggestions of evidence that show the competence in practice. We have linked each set of competencies (or capacities) to items on the supervision checklist.

Overall

Throughout the supervisor-coach relationship, the supervisor utilizes:

- integrity, rapport and flexibility;
- their ability to handle complexity;
- a co-creative approach;
- an equal, OK-OK alliance;
- meta-perspective thinking;
- respect for individuality and diversity;
- simultaneous engagement and detachment – 'unattached intimacy';
- a psychological framework for an understanding of process and content.

These will be shown by the supervisor, for example:

- inviting mutual Adult-to-Adult relating;
- nurturing the relationship with the coach and recognising that it is at the heart of learning;
- trusting in a mutual state of awareness that arises in the moment and out of open conversation;
- staying comfortable with 'not knowing' as one of the best states to expand awareness;
- being willing to be vulnerable, and fostering an environment where the coach can be vulnerable;
- consistently listening, with open curiosity, at the logical, emotional and systemic levels;
- sharing what s/he notices about the coach and their situation.

From the supervision checklist, this demonstrates 'equal relationship' and 'supervisor models process': the supervisor also pays attention to balancing the various aspects of the supervision.

Management/accountability/coach as professional

The supervisor

- sets context and attends to boundaries (e.g. coaching/mentoring);
- is clear about their own stance and values;
- is aware of ethical issues; alerts and holds the coach to them;
- makes and honours multi-party contracts;
- establishes safety and protection for the coach and their clients;
- works to agreed goals;
- refers on when appropriate;
- agrees the level and limits of confidentiality;
- thinks systemically and stays aware of contextual influences;

- takes account of organisational and community perspectives;
- self-manages, including getting own supervision and time for reflection and development.

By, for instance,

- co-creatively helping the coach identify what they want to accomplish – overall and within each session;
- checking regularly on the supervisory relationship with the coach and making new agreements on how best they can work together;
- respectfully naming inconsistency or lack of congruence.

From the checklist, this demonstrates 'contract fulfilled' and the 'reduction of probability of harm'.

Support/nurture/coach as person

The supervisor

- focuses attention on coach's needs;
- maintains positive, affirming approach;
- gives permission to be with what is, i.e. the coach's 'map';
- works with ambiguity, paradox and uncertainty;
- uses intuition effectively;
- establishes trust, contact and intimacy;
- values own response as material for learning ('use of self');
- identifies, names and works with parallel process;
- keeps psychological level 'clean';
- recognises 'patterns' in coach and self;
- gets own support.

By, for instance,

- being observant, empathetic, and responsive to the coach and to how they learn, and to what they want to learn;
- being fully present, in the here-and-now and attuned to the moment, supporting the coach in shifting attention from 'out there' to 'in here';
- noticing and exploring energy shifts;
- exploring beliefs, behaviours, emotions, language, tone of voice, pace of speech and inflection, as appropriate;
- listening for strengths and resources as well as limiting beliefs: listening is cumulative, from interaction to interaction;
- seeking to understand the coach's context and perspectives;
- inviting exploration into the coach's process as well as the content of discussion.

From the checklist, this indicates 'identification of key issues'.

Development/transformation/coach as coach

The supervisor

- identifies underlying issues for the coach, brings them into awareness;
- intervenes appropriately for the coach's stage of development ('functions within supervision');
- notes changes in the coach's knowledge, skills and awareness and promotes development;
- integrates a 'theory to practice' approach;
- gives objective feedback and critique on practice and encourages learning;
- includes systemic thinking and cultural awareness;
- promotes reflection, active experimentation and self-discovery;
- invites Adult awareness and solution-focus;
- challenges actively and appropriately in order to promote growth;
- encourages the coach to use a wide range of perspectives;
- maintains their own ongoing development and professional competence.

By, for instance,

- exploring what is important or meaningful to the coach around what they want to accomplish in the session;
- being open to challenging and changing in new ways, using subjective experience in co-creating new learnings as well as being engaged in those of the coach;
- exploring the 'relational field' with curiosity as a potential source of data;
- surfacing patterns of relating with others and exploring them with curiosity;
- bringing questions and observations emerging from what the coach is learning about themselves;
- sharing observations, intuitions, comments, thoughts and feelings, to serve the coach's learning or forward movement – without any attachment to being right;
- demonstrating relational experiences that provide empowering new learning;
- 'exploring for learning', more than 'inquiring for solutioning';
- noting questions, intuitions and observations to create new learning;
- being curious about the relational field and what is happening in the here-and-now.

From the checklist, these actions and interventions will 'increase developmental direction'.

We offer these competencies as prompts to reflection on what is required and expected of coach supervisors.

Codes for ethical practice

A number of coaching organisations have ethical codes available to access online:

The European Mentoring and Coaching Council and the Association for Coaching have a joint code:

www.emccuk.org

and

www.associationforcoaching.com/pages/about/code-ethics-good-practice

The Association for Professional Executive Coaching and Supervision (APECS) and the Association of Coach Supervisors also publish ethical codes at:

www.apecs.org

and

www.associationofcoachingsupervisors.com

The International Coach Federation code of ethics can be found at:

www.coachfederation.org/about/ethics

and

www.coachfederation.org.uk

The European Association for Transactional Analysis (EATA) has developed an extensive document on ethics, including definitions, assumptions, goals, values, principles and a grid for assessing ethical practice. It gives an excellent overview of ethics in professional contexts, and can be accessed at:

www.eatanews.org/eata-2/ethics/

The International Transactional Analysis Association (ITAA) has largely adopted the EATA code. It can be found at:

http://itaaworld.org/itaa-governance-documents

Further reading

Coach supervision books

There are not so many books on coach supervision that we can suggest a long list for further reading! These are some we have found helpful, for various reasons, as we explain below:

On Being a Supervisee: Creating learning partnerships, Michael Carroll and Maria Gilbert (London: Vukani Publishing, 2005). An invaluable guide to the whole business of supervision (for any field, though primarily written for counsellors and therapists), it aims to explore the supervisee's perspective, based on the premise that supervision is about learning – and that supervisees can be enabled to get the most out of the experience by understanding this perspective.

Coaching, Mentoring and Organisational Consultancy: Supervision and development, Peter Hawkins and Nick Smith (London: Open University Press, 2006). A source of information and reference as well as newer ideas with a focus on the business world, this includes material originally published in Hawkins and Robin Shohet's classic *Supervision in the Helping Professions* and adds much more.

Reflective Practice and Supervision for Coaches, Julie Hay (London: Open University Press, 2007). Well structured and clear, this is a comprehensive manual using a number of TA concepts to help coaches and supervisors improve their practice by understanding the underlying dynamic.

Coaching and Mentoring Supervision: Theory and practice, Tatiana Bachkirova, David Clutterbuck and Peter Jackson (London: Open University Press, 2011). This is a definitive text, covering the latest thinking, models and approaches by some expert practitioners in coaching and mentoring supervision.

TA books

If our use of TA as a way of understanding self and others has piqued your interest, and you want to learn more, these books offer distinctive approaches designed for different contexts – all of them by leading TA writers:

Into TA: A comprehensive textbook on transactional analysis, William Cornell, Anne de Graaf, Trudi Newton and Moniek Thunnissen (London: Karnac, 2016).

Into TA is a new and comprehensive textbook of contemporary transactional analysis in theory and practice. The first section of the book focuses on theory, presented so that both beginning and experienced professionals will find much of value. TA theory is then further integrated with other current models of psychology, education, and organisational consultation. The second section provides examples of TA in practice that brings the theory to life.

An Introduction to Transactional Analysis, Phil Lapworth and Charlotte Sills (London: Sage, 2011). This book introduces the theory and practice of TA from a uniquely relational perspective. It is illustrated throughout with examples of TA used in executive coaching.

Working It Out at Work: Understanding attitudes and building relationships, Julie Hay (Watford: Sherwood Publishing, 1993). A prime resource on TA for people in organisations. It includes lively and accessible explanations of theory, together with an emphasis on using the ideas in working with others.

TACTICS: Transactional analysis concepts for all trainers, teachers and tutors + insight into collaborative learning strategies, Rosemary Napper and Trudi Newton (Ipswich: TA Resources, 2nd edition 2014). With an accessible and coherent approach that can enhance the effectiveness of relational learning, this is a uniquely practical guide for professionals such as mentors, coaches, trainers, tutors, lecturers and facilitators, whose role involves enabling others to learn. With reflective exercises and ideas for application alongside current learning theory, it focuses on how TA can be used to inform the process of adult learning.

Bibliography

Bachkirova, T., Clutterbuck, D., and Jackson, P. (2011) *Coaching and Mentoring Supervision: Theory and practice (Supervision in Context)*, London: Open University Press.

Barrow, G. (2011) 'Educator as Cultivator', *Transactional Analysis Journal*, 41: 308–14.

Barrow, G., Bradshaw, E., and Newton, T. (2001) *Improving Behaviour and Raising Self-Esteem in the Classroom: A practical guide to using TA*, London: David Fulton.

Beinart, H. and Clohessy, S (2017) *Effective Supervisory Relationships*, Chichester: John Wiley.

Berne, E. (1961) *Transactional Analysis in Psychotherapy: A systemic and social psychiatry*, New York: Grove Press.

Berne, E. (1963) *Structure and Dynamics of Organisations and Groups*, New York: Ballantine Books.

Berne, E. (1966) *Principles of Group Treatment*, New York: Grove Press.

Campos, L. (2013) Personal communication, 5 April.

Carroll, M. (2001) 'The Spirituality of Supervision', in Carroll and Tholstrup, eds, *Integrative Approaches to Supervision*, London: Jessica Kingsley.

Carroll, M. (2013) *Ethical Maturity in the Helping Professions: Making difficult life and work decisions*, London: Jessica Kingsley.

Carroll, M., and Gilbert, M. (2005) *On Being a Supervisee: Creating learning partnerships*, London: Vukani Publishing.

Choy, A. (1990) 'The Winners Triangle', *Transactional Analysis Journal*, 20: 40–6.

Clarke, J. I. (1996) 'The Synergistic Use of Five Transactional Analysis Concepts by Educators', *Transactional Analysis Journal*, 26: 214–19.

Clarke, J. I., and Dawson, C. (1998) *Growing Up Again: Parenting ourselves, parenting our children*, Center City: Hazelden.

Clarkson, P. (1991) 'Group Imago and the Stages of Group Development', *Transactional Analysis Journal*, 21: 36–50.

Clarkson, P. (1992) *Transactional Analysis Psychotherapy: An integrated approach*, London: Routledge.

Clarkson, P. (1994) *The Achilles Syndrome*, Shaftesbury: Element Books.

Cochrane, H., and Newton, T. (2011) *Supervision for Coaches: A guide to thoughtful work*, Ipswich: Supervision for Coaches Publishing.

Cornell, W. (2006) 'Roundtable on the Ethics of Relational Transactional Analysis', *Transactional Analysis Journal*, 36: 105–19.

Cornell, W., and Shadbolt, C. (2007) 'Live and in Limbo: A case study of an in-person transactional analysis consultation', *Transactional Analysis Journal,* 37: 159–71.

Cox, E., Bachkirova, T., and Clutterbuck, D., eds. (2014) *The Complete Handbook of Coaching* (2nd edn), London: Sage.

Cox, M. (1999) 'The Relationship between Ego State Structure and Function: A diagrammatic formulation, *Transactional Analysis Journal* 29: 49–58.

Cox, M. (2007) 'On Doing Supervision', *Transactional Analysis Journal,* 37: 104–14.

Cupitt, D. (1988) *The New Christian Ethics,* London: SCM Press.

De Graaf, A., and Levy, J. (2011) 'Business As Usual: Ethics in the fast-changing and complex world of organizations', *Transactional Analysis Journal,* 41: 123–8.

Dekoninck, J. (1994) Unpublished Workshop Material, ARIATE: Paris.

Drego, P. (1983) 'The Cultural Parent', *Transactional Analysis Journal,* 13: 224–7.

Drego, P. (2006) 'Freedom and Responsibility: Social empowerment and the altruistic model of ego states', *Transactional Analysis Journal,* 36: 90–104.

Drego, P. (2009) 'Bonding the Ethnic Child with the Universal Parent: Strategies and ethos of a transactional analysis ecocommunity activist', *Transactional Analysis Journal,* 39: 193–206.

EATA (2012) *Ethics Code Updated.* Available at www.eatanews.org/eata-2/ethics/ (accessed 23 March 2017).

English, F. (1975) 'The Three-Cornered Contract', *Transactional Analysis Journal,* 5: 383–4.

Erskine, R. (1982) 'Supervision of Psychotherapy: Models for professional development', *Transactional Analysis Journal,* 12: 314–21.

Erskine, R. (2002) 'Relational Needs', *EATA Newsletter,* 73: 5–9.

Eusden, S. (2011) 'Minding the Gap: Ethical considerations for therapeutic engagement', *Transactional Analysis Journal,* 41: 101–13.

Fowlie, H., and Sills, C., eds. (2011) *Relational Transactional Analysis: Principles in practice,* London: Karnac.

Freire, P., and Ramos, M. (1973; 2nd edn revised, 1996) *Pedagogy of the Oppressed,* London: Penguin Education.

Gerhardt, S. (2004) *Why Love Matters: How affection shapes a baby's brain,* Hove: Brunner-Routledge.

Gopnik, A., Meltzoff, A.N., and Kuhl, P. (1999) *The Scientist in the Crib,* New York: Morrow.

Hampson, D. (1998) 'The Tactile Imago', *INTAND Newsletter,* 6:1.

Hawkins, P., and Shohet, S. (1996; revised edn 2006) *Supervision in the Helping Professions,* London: Open University Press.

Hawkins, P., and Smith, N. (2006) *Coaching, Mentoring and Organisational Consultancy: Supervision and development,* London: Open University Press.

Hay, J. (1993) *Working It Out at Work: Understanding attitudes and building relationships',* Watford: Sherwood Publishing.

Hay, J. (2007) *Reflective Practice and Supervision for Coaches,* London: Open University Press.

Horton M., and Freire, P. (1991) *We Make the Road by Walking: Conversations on education and social change,* Philadelphia: Temple University Press.

James, M., and Jongeward, D. (1971) *Born to Win: Transactional analysis with gestalt experiments,* Reading: Addison Wesley.

Joines, V., and Stewart, I. (2002) *Personality Adaptations: A new guide to human understanding in psychotherapy and counselling*, Nottingham: Lifespace.

Kadushin, A., and Harkness, D. (1976; 4th edn 2002) *Supervision in Social Work*, New York: Columbia University Press.

Karpman, S. (1968) 'Fairy Tales and Script Drama Analysis', *Transactional Analysis Bulletin*, 7: (26) 39–43.

Kolb, D. (1984) *Experiential Learning: Experience as the source of learning and development*, Englewood Cliffs: Prentice Hall.

Lahad, M. (2000) *Creative Supervision: The use of expressive arts methods in supervision and self-supervision*, London: Jessica Kingsley.

Lapworth, P., and Sills, C. (2011) *An Introduction to Transactional Analysis*, London: Sage.

Le Guernic, A. (2004) 'Fairy Tales and Psychological Life Plans', *Transactional Analysis Journal*, 34: 216–22.

Levin-Landheer, P. (1982) 'The Cycle of Development', *Transactional Analysis Journal*, 12: 129–39.

Marum, P. (2015, personal communication) *Differences between Supervision, Mentoring and Coaching*, Lexington: ICF.

Mazzetti, M. (2007) 'Supervision in Transactional Analysis: An operational model', *Transactional Analysis Journal*, 37: 93–103.

Mezirow, J. (2000) *Learning as Transformation*, San Francisco: Jossey Bass.

Micholt, N. (1992) 'Psychological Distance and Group Interventions', *Transactional Analysis Journal*, 22: 228–33.

Miljkovic, N. (2016) 'Relational Needs in Education', in Barrow, G., and Newton, T. (eds) *Educational Transactional Analysis: An international guide to theory & practice*, London: Routledge.

Napper, R., and Newton, T. (2000; 2nd edn 2014) *Tactics: Transactional analysis concepts for all trainers, teachers and tutors + insight into collaborative learning strategies*, Ipswich: TA Resources.

Napper, R., and Newton, T. (2014) 'Transactional Analysis and Coaching', in Cox, E., Bachkirova, T., and Clutterbuck D. (eds) *The Complete Handbook of Coaching*, London: Sage.

Newton, T. (2003) 'Identifying Educational Philosophy and Practice through Imagoes in Transactional Analysis Training Groups', *Transactional Analysis Journal*, 33: 321–31.

Newton, T. (2006) 'Script, Psychological Life Plans and the Learning Cycle', *Transactional Analysis Journal*, 36: 186–95.

Newton, T. (2012) 'The Supervision Triangle: An integrating model', *Transactional Analysis Journal*, 42: 103–9.

Newton, T. (2013) 'Why I Write', *The Script (Newsletter of the ITAA)*, 43: 4, 6–7.

Newton, T., and Napper, R. (2007) 'The Bigger Picture: Supervision as an educational framework for all fields', *Transactional Analysis Journal* 37: 150–8.

Proctor, B. (2000) *Group supervision: A guide to creative practice*, London: Sage.

Remen R. N. (1989) 'The Search for Healing', in Carlson, R., and Shield, B. (eds) *Healers on Healing*, Los Angeles: Tarcher.

Rilke, R. M. (2016) *Letters to a Young Poet*, London: Penguin Classics.

Rogers, C. (1961) *On Becoming a Person*, London: Constable.

Rushdie, S. (1991) 'Excerpts from Rushdie's Address: 1,000 days "trapped inside a metaphor"', *New York Times*. 12 December.

Schmid, B. (1994) 'Transactional Analysis and Social Roles', republished in Mohr, G., and Steinert, T. eds (2008) *Growth and Change for Organisations: Transactional analysis – new developments 1995–2006*, Pleasonton: ITAA.

Schulz, K. (2010) *Being Wrong: Adventures in the margin of error*, London: Portobello.

Searles, H. (1955) 'The Informational Value of the Supervisor's Emotional Experience', in *Collected Papers on Schizophrenia and Related Subjects*, London: Hogarth Press.

Shmukler, D. (2011) 'The Use of Self in Psychotherapy: Key-note address, London IARTA Conference', in Fowlie, H., and Sills, C. eds, *Relational Transactional Analysis: Principles in practice*, London: Karnac.

Sills, C., and Mazzetti, M. (2009) 'The Comparative Script System: A tool for developing supervisors', *Transactional Analysis Journal*, 39: 305–14.

Steiner, C. (1974) *Scripts People Live*, New York: Grove Press.

Steare, R. (2008; 5th edn 2013) *Ethicability: How to decide what's right and find the courage to do it*, Tonbridge: Roger Steare Consulting.

Stoltenberg, C. S., and Delworth, U. (1987) *Supervising Counsellors and Therapists: A developmental approach*, San Francisco: Josey-Bass Wiley.

Temple, S. (1999) 'Functional Fluency for Educational Transactional Analysts', *Transactional Analysis Journal*, 29: 164–74.

Tudor, K. (2003) 'The Neopsyche: The integrating adult ego state', in Sills, C., and Hargaden, H., eds, *Key Concepts in Transactional Analysis; Contemporary Views: Egostates*, London: Worth.

Tudor, K., and Summers, G. (2014) *Co-creative Transactional Analysis*, London: Karnac.

Tuckman, B., and Jensen, K. (1977) 'Stages of Small Group Development', *Journal of Group and Organisational Studies*, 2.

Ware, P. (1983) 'Personality Adaptations (Doors to Therapy)', *Transactional Analysis Journal*, 13: 11–19.

Zull, J. (2002) *The Art of Changing the Brain: Enriching the practice of teaching by exploring the biology of learning*, Sterling: Stylus.

Index

Note: Italicised numbers refer to diagrams